ONE LIGHT

Jon Whistler

ONE LIGHT
REPRINTING 2016

First Published 1996
Second Printing 1998
Revised Edition 2005
Fourth Printing 2016

PUBLISHER'S NOTE

Since the first publishing in 1996, ONE LIGHT has inspired other labors by the author, and some associated works. Jon Whistler has brought to us further transmissions in ENTER THE VORTEX AS ONE LIGHT; the ORACLE TO FREEDOM; and THE THREAD OF INFINITY. All the wondrous truths in these books have led the consciousness of many to experience greater self-healing and Freedom in Light.

But ONE LIGHT is the first. And being first, it's a lot more than just a book. It's a door. By the time you turn the last page you will understand that you are now on the way to a great adventure – the journey to YOU – and that ONE LIGHT is the key to your freedom from illusion and the key to your Joy in Light.

The Publisher

Foreword

To some readers this book may appear to be fantasy or science fiction. I can assure you that it is not. After having lived through the experiences described, and having seen the horror of what some of the Earth's 'ruling' class are doing to this planet, I can say from my heart that we NEED to face what this book proposes. We NEED to make a turnabout in our consciousness.

This is not a channeled work, in the sense of channeling. The mysterious object discovered at Pallett Creek in 1994 provided the message which follows. I recorded it as it came and have reproduced the transcripts faithfully in this book.

This book holds a powerful meaning for Mankind. How often have you questioned who or what you really are? Most of the time you encourage answers that have been offered by others – the religious answer, the intellectual or materialistic answer, the mystical answer.

Why are you living this life? What do you expect after you die? To most people life seems pointless. What about the planet you live on? Is it only an inert mass of minerals? Or is it a living organism ascending into the light of its own nature? Are you assisting its ascension? Or are you helping to destroy it?

This book could be termed the doorway to the New Cosmology. I know that once you experience its revelations you will never be the same again. I know I wasn't.

Jon Whistler, 1995.

Prologue

One hot summer's afternoon, on a Friday in June, something happened which was to change my life and the lives of two others, forever. Four days earlier, I had managed to dig up out of the earth the strangest and most frustrating unknown object I had ever encountered. In my time as a geologist I have frequently come across interesting or unusual finds. Often they were archeological – arrow heads or bits of broken pottery. I have even found the odd bone or two, although I have never been lucky enough to discover any dinosaur remains. Once I picked up an intriguing crystal that even I could not identify. I kept it for a while and tried to find out what it was; then it seemed that it started to have a disturbing effect on me so I gave it away.

This latest find was a real puzzle however. My two colleagues and I were absolutely stumped as to its identity.

It was an artifact, a cylindrical object shaped like a capsule and totally solid. By its smooth, shiny, unmarked appearance it had to be of modern manufacture. But could we tell what it was? The hell we couldn't!

Hence the frustration, that and the fact that, although the thing was seamless and solid it reminded us all so much of a container that we reckoned it ought to be hollow and there should be something inside. And could we get it open? No way!

Then on the Friday it happened. Our journey began into mystery, into a vortex of Inter-dimensional power, which pulled us toward an inexorable destiny from which there has been, and ever will be, *no return.*

Without any warning and all by itself, the capsule (as we had decided to term it) began to change character. Then the 'fun' began.

I fell back into my chair. The light from the capsule was so intense that my eyes began to ache. Moving my hands in front of them to shield them, I thought: My God, this damned thing has blinded us; now all that's left is the explosion!

Before I could do or think anything else, a strange sensation began moving up my spine. It was terrifying, a fierce burning that rose like liquid fire, as if my vertebrae formed a channel of lava that surged into my skull. When it reached the crown of my head I experienced a violent pain, as though my head was about to explode. It felt like every one of my brain cells was firing high voltage electrical impulses, shooting like stars, like lightning flashes across the chasms of my synapses.

Through my pain I heard Rose scream. I was helpless. I could not move to save her or myself. All three of us were trapped inside the weirdest, most uncomfortable of happenings. But just what was happening?

Stunned and suffering, I stayed frozen for what seemed an eternity, then the pain began to diminish and the light intensity decreased. Gradually my sight began to return. It was like coming out of anesthesia, everything blurry and surreal. I could see Rose slumped in her chair. Carl was on the floor. He had never made it to the door.

'What happened?' I croaked, but no one answered. Possibly I had begun to recover before either of them. I stared at the capsule. The sun still shone on it, but it was glowing with a soft blue light. I moved toward it. As I put my fingers close I could feel a strong heat intensity radiating from it. I decided that it was best left alone. Rose seemed to be coming around and Carl was dragging himself up from the floor. I helped him to his chair and looked to see if Rose was okay.

Once he was near enough to normal, Carl asked: 'What are we going to do now? I don't think that thing is a bomb, but it sure gives you a headache.'

We all glared somewhat resentfully at the capsule, when abruptly it began to pulsate.

'I'm out of here!' Carl shouted. He tried to leave but somehow his feet and brain would not coordinate and he slipped back to the floor.

Very quickly a brilliant blue light filled the room. The color could best be described as an electric blue, and we stared at one another through its vividness like amazed children. My pulses were racing, yet, conversely, inside me was a deep feeling of peace. I could not explain that feeling, only some intuition told me that no harm would come to us from the capsule. At last it seemed possible to breathe and relax. I wondered if the others were feeling the same way.

We stood in that marvelous blue atmosphere, and from within the center of the capsule a bright, fiery light began to emanate.

'What next?' whispered Rose, and we all three tended to back off a little, just in case…

The fiery light danced on the space of the table just in front of the capsule until it seemed to coalesce into a small cloud of moving embers. The light then organized itself, became vaguely recognizable. A form, a shape: a human-like form two feet high, of pure light, around its 'head' was 'hair' like the corona of the sun, and beaming from the 'head' two 'eyes' glowing like orange fire.

A holographic image!

I had seen holograms before, but this one was sensational!

I gaped stupidly at it. It was almost too amazing to believe!

Dear God, have we dug up an alien after all? I thought.

Then came the second shock, more staggering than the first. The hologram spoke!

CHAPTER 1

The Discovery

I have spent most of my working life in geological research. As a boy I grew up in a town just north of Cape Mendocino in northern California. I was always interested in earthquakes and, like most Californians, respected and feared them. When you live in earthquake country you have to be prepared twenty four hours a day, because you have little or no warning of their coming. I suppose that is why I studied geology, as I felt that there must be some way that we could predict them and prevent unnecessary tragedy.

After graduating from Humboldt State University, I worked with various research groups, and later joined the United States Geological Survey. Most of what I did involved measuring for early warning systems. I liked the work, as it provided me with the opportunity of getting outside in the open air. I do not particularly like being cooped up in air conditioned offices.

There is quite a lot of data published on the tectonic plates in the San Francisco area, but little attention has been paid to a major fault pattern just south of where I lived as a kid. It is termed 'triple junction', because it is a point where three plates meet. These are the Pacific, the North American and the Gorda plates.

The Gorda is sub-ducting, or diving, east beneath the North American plate, and is also being butted from the south by the encroaching San Andreas system. Generally we consider this spot to be one of the most seismically tortured in California.

The greatest hazards seen in this area are the sub-duction earthquakes, which are generated as the Gorda plate thrusts beneath the coast. Sub-duction quakes are the largest on Earth. The last one on Cape Mendocino was in 1992 near triple junction and was 7.2 on the R scale, and it was quite a shake.

Although there seems to be a lot of fear attached to earthquakes, most Californians take the shakes in their stride. Quakes are occurring more frequently around the world, especially on the Pacific Rim. A while back the USGS flew me to Australia to do some research on the quake in Newcastle, as that baby was one of the most recent in that area of the Pacific.

My latest project was a 'dig' on the San Andreas Fault at Pallett Creek, about thirty miles north east of Los Angeles, and I had been working that area since the LA earthquake in January 1994. By 'dig' I mean just that – digging trenches down into the history of Mother Earth in order to date the periods between quakes. It's all there, in the soil – a thousand years of evidence, deposited in the layers of peat from the time when Pallett Creek was a swamp. The peat is great because it contains carbon and we can use radio carbon dating to determine its age within a few decades. Earthquake activity shows up as an offset in the peat layers, so timing its occurrence and measuring the size of the individual quake is not too difficult.

The idea of the Survey is to be able to predict the frequency of earthquakes in a specific area by dating the periods between past upheavals. Ten feet into the soil and we can date and measure as far back as 1265. Just south east of Pallett Creek, near the town of Wrightwood, we have already underscored a threat along this stretch of the San Andreas, and we predict it to go in the next thirty years and to be around 7.9 on the R scale.

I guess that is why I have always considered my work to be important and worthwhile, since lives and property could be riding on the information we gather.

At forty five, life had been fairly good to me, except for a divorce ten years back. I had been in my job with the USGS for many years and enjoyed it, and my health was fine, or what I then considered to be fine – I know better now. I didn't mind a Millers or two when I watched Monday night football, as it was a regular thing to do.

Only my social calendar left something to be desired. I suppose I am a quiet kind of guy, no great party animal, and most of my satisfaction in life came from my work. I got on well with my colleagues – I headed up a team, and never had much conflict of personality with any of my peers or subordinates.

At Pallett Creek there were three of us working. Carl Reisenger was from San Francisco. He had been associated with me on various research teams in the past, but for all that I knew very little about him. He was a few years older than myself, a thin nervous looking man with dark greying hair. A loner, reticent and somewhat cold, he never gave much of himself to others. He was okay, but not really my type of person.

The other team member was Rose Medlin, from Scottsdale, Arizona. New to the Survey, she had been graduated from University for six years. Prior to that, she had been researching with her old university. She was part Hopi Indian, with the strong attractive features characteristic of the race. I liked Rose, and the reliable, calm nature she possessed. She had a wicked sense of humor too sometimes. She seemed to like me; we were always pretty easy in each other's company.

On the whole our team worked well together. Carl, with his silences, nevertheless was an honest, efficient worker who always did his share, and Rose added a touch of lightness and good feeling, necessary when things got a bit heavy or too tedious. I found the work mostly calming and soothing, which is rather ironic in retrospect. A man who grounds his life in the study of the Earth's disastrous upheavals and finds it restful is bound fairly soon to be jolted awake by a shock. Little did I know then what a shock it would be – a quake of major proportions – in my heart and mind as well as in my every day existence. Like a lightning bolt out of the blue empty sky.

The first tremors in consciousness began one hot Monday morning about three weeks after we had been working the current site. I was busy clearing away some scrub and top soil for a new trench. In the heat I sweated badly and my back felt a bit achy from all the bending.

A thought wandered in – I'm too old for this. Maybe it's time I gave it up and went and sat on a beach somewhere – when I turned over a clod of earth and saw, glinting in the sunlight, the curved end of something shiny. Curious and unaccountably excited, I dug further. The thing was a metallic blue in color and was shaped like a capsule similar to those used by drug companies, except that it was about two feet long and eight inches in diameter. In spite of having been buried in the earth, it had not a mark on it, only a little dust. I stared at it for some time before I picked it up, I don't know why, and touched it cautiously; thinking that it might be hot in the sun, but it was not. Cool as night and much lighter in weight than I would have guessed. Extremely so; much less than half a pound.

I thought: How did this sucker get here? Then a curious emotion tickled my consciousness – something like fearful anticipation mixed with great joy. I could not explain the feeling, so I passed it off. I called out to the others who were working not far away.

'What the heck do you think this is?'

'I wondered what you were doing, staring at the ground like that,' said Carl as he came over. Rose followed. 'I thought he was trying to hypnotize a rattler,' she said dryly.

'Here, catch!'

I tossed the object in Carl's direction. He caught it like a football pro but his face showed surprise.

It was obvious he had expected it to be heavy.

'Strange thing. I wonder what it is?' he said. 'Doesn't seem like it has any archaeological value, it's quite new looking.'

'Wow,' said Rose. 'Let me look.'

Carl handed it to her. She stroked the smooth surface as if it was a cat. 'Mm,' she murmured, 'it's beautiful. Can I have it?'

I knew she was teasing. I took the shining object and put it in my specimen bag. 'We'll take it back to the site office and then we can look at in more detail.'

'And shade,' added Rose.

Around noon we were back at the site office and less interested in our lunch than in the mysterious object on the table.

We all inspected it with great interest. 'It's like a time capsule,' said Rose, 'but it's too light to have anything much in it.'

'A time capsule?' scoffed Carl. 'It has no joins – no top, no bottom, no lid. It's difficult to see just how it was sealed, and it seems to have practically no mass.' He then took out his hammer and began to gently chip at the outside of the thing. The hammer made no marks or scratches to the surface. 'This baby is tough.'

'It still could be a capsule,' Rose replied. 'Maybe it's from outer space.' Carl sneered. 'And pigs may fly.'

Rose frowned at him, and I decided to calm the waters. 'We'll agree to call it a capsule then.

However, we seem to be getting nowhere with this line of investigation. I don't think we should rush this. Let's keep it quiet for now. It may be of some value to science, but we don't want the press to be involved. They always blow everything out of proportion.'

During the following days we performed acid tests to the surface, compression tests to look for joins, and anything else we could think of to get that capsule to reveal its secrets. We did everything except X/ray it, only because we did not have the equipment.

By Thursday we were desperate for an answer. More frustrated than desperate I think, because the damned thing wouldn't budge. Also it worried us that with the weekend coming up we still wouldn't have gotten anywhere and we had to decide what to do. In the back of our minds was the notion that if this capsule, or whatever it was, proved to be something unique and valuable, then we would need to be able to protect our rights of discovery. We agreed then that Friday afternoon was to be the deadline – we would decide one way or another, the fate of the capsule.

CHAPTER 2

The Opening

It was just noon when we returned to the site office on Friday. It had been another hot morning with the temperature hitting ninety-six degrees Fahrenheit, and we were glad to get inside, as the small air conditioning unit on the office window made the room more bearable than the day outside.

We sat down to talk about the unknown capsule that somehow had come into our lives. We did not just want to hand it over and lose whatever gains we could realize from the discovery. I suppose we are all somewhat mercenary; but, what the heck, you have to protect your own patch.

But obviously caring nothing for our ambitions or frustrations, the object of our discussion lay on the specimen table, as mute and mysterious as the day I found it. I glanced at it briefly; its simple presence seemed to mock our futile efforts.

Hating to admit defeat, I turned away, when out of the corner of my eye I saw what I thought to be a glowing in the center of the capsule. However I put it down to the reflection of the sun casting its rays on the capsule through the window.

This was not so, for as I looked again at the capsule I felt that the light from the sun was affecting it and there was a definite alteration in the character of the surface. The capsule was glowing; something weird was occurring, I knew.

Wonder turned to sudden fear. What if this innocent looking object was a new-fangled kind of bomb? And what if it was set to go off after a certain exposure to light or heat? I said as much, and the others stared wide-eyed, first at the capsule, then at me.

Courageously Carl jumped to his feet. 'I'll throw it outside!'

When his hand touched the capsule he recoiled with a scream. 'It burned me! It's boiling!' 'Let's get out of here!'

As Rose and I got up to run to the door, the capsule radiated a brilliant light like the sun that, in fact, blinded us. It was instantaneous and totally disabling.

I fell back into my chair. The light from the capsule was so intense that my eyes began to ache.

Moving my hands in front of them to shield them, I thought: My God, this damned thing has blinded us; now all that's left is the explosion!

Before I could do or think anything else, a strange sensation began moving up my spine. It was terrifying – a fierce burning that rose like liquid fire, as if my vertebrae formed a channel of lava that surged into my skull. When it reached the crown of my head I experienced a violent pain, as though my head was about to explode. It felt like every one of my brain cells was firing high voltage electrical impulses – shooting like stars, like lightning flashes across the chasms of my synapses.

Through my pain I heard Rose scream. I was helpless. I could not move to save her or myself. All three of us were trapped inside the weirdest, most uncomfortable of happenings. But just what was happening?

Stunned and suffering, I stayed frozen for what seemed an eternity, then the pain began to diminish and the light intensity decreased. Gradually my sight began to return. It was like coming out of anesthesia, everything blurry and surreal. I could see Rose slumped in her chair. Carl was on the floor. He had never made it to the door.

'What happened?' I croaked, but no one answered. Possibly I had begun to recover before either of them. I stared at the capsule. The sun still shone on it, but it was glowing with a soft blue light. I moved toward it. As I put my fingers close I could feel a strong heat intensity radiating from it. I decided that it was best left alone. Rose seemed to be coming around and Carl was dragging himself up from the floor. I helped him to his chair and looked to see if Rose was okay.

Once he was near enough to normal, Carl asked: 'What are we going to do now? I don't think that thing is a bomb, but it sure gives you a headache.'

We all glared somewhat resentfully at the capsule, when abruptly it began to pulsate.

'I'm out of here!' Carl shouted. He tried to leave but somehow his feet and brain would not coordinate and he slipped back to the floor.

Very quickly a brilliant blue light filled the room. The color could best be described as an electric blue, and we stared at one another through its vividness like amazed children. My pulses were racing, yet, conversely, inside me was a deep feeling of peace. I could not explain that feeling, only some intuition told me that no harm would come to us from the capsule. At last it seemed possible to breathe and relax. I wondered if the others were feeling the same way.

We stood in that marvelous blue atmosphere, and from within the center of the capsule a bright, fiery light began to emanate.

'What next?' whispered Rose, and we all three tended to back off a little, just in case…

The fiery light danced on the space of the table just in front of the capsule until it seemed to coalesce into a small cloud of moving embers. The light then organized itself, became vaguely recognizable. A form, a shape: a human-like form two feet high, of pure light, around its 'head' was 'hair' like the corona of the sun, and beaming from the 'head' two 'eyes' glowing like orange fire.

A holographic image!

I had seen holograms before, but this one was sensational! I gaped stupidly at it. It was almost too amazing to believe!

Dear God, have we dug up an alien after all? I thought.

Then came the second shock, more staggering than the first. The hologram spoke!

And in our language! Dumbly I glanced at Rose and Carl. Was it truly speaking aloud or was this a fantasy of my embattled senses?

But clearly the thing had spoken. The others' faces were rapt in attention as they listened, and this is the substance of what we all heard:

'I am Zadore, keeper of Solar Gate. I have sent this capsule to Earth to awaken Mankind to the destruction it is causing to the Planet Earth. You, Mankind, have forgotten why you came to this planet and what your original purpose was. In your sickness you are now approaching a time in the Earth's consciousness where, if you do not awaken to your destructive habits, you and those who willfully work to destroy the planet will meet your own destruction and live in the darkness for many millennia.

Soon I will send a Vortex of Light and Healing that will allow those who are now awakening their consciousness to higher dimensions to move through the Vortex to the Light of their own being.

Listen and I will enlighten your hearts and minds so that this message will reach out to those who are ready to seek the change. The days of your continual destructiveness are numbered.

Take heed of my warning!'

Zadore then spoke on the consciousness of the Planet Earth:

'**Y**our Light Essence is now trapped in your Earthly body, and you have forgotten your birthright. This capture of consciousness is a direct result of some perverse beings who came to the Earth dimension many thousands of years ago. In the passing of time these beings have succeeded in mastering the art of manipulating the energies that underlie the essence of the planet.

Your own essence or light frequency belongs to the star system, which, at the command of the Higher Dimensional Light Beings, directed that the Earth receive energies necessary to empower it with the Light and Consciousness of the Galaxy. This was to assist the Earth in its elevation to the position of a conscious star in this ever expanding Galaxy.

Thus the radiant beams of light from the various star systems were focused through the Sun and directed to the Earth, grounding the light frequencies into human organisms or bodies. So the Earth's consciousness is seeded by the light and consciousness of the Galaxy, and that light is the light which is YOU.

Once your light rays were grounded through the lowest frequency, which is termed Ego, your consciousness was directed to your new found freedom, or separation. Due to the attractive power of the physical senses of the body into which your consciousness is projected, you fell in love with the illusion of separateness, and that illusion has been woven into the DNA structure of the Earth-body you now inhabit. You have forgotten your original purpose, and have been trapped in this illusion of power and separateness.

The perverse control beings, of which I spoke earlier, have

11

chosen to call themselves Astral Lords, and when they move their consciousness through an Earth-body it is always to draw greater power and energy from a captive consciousness such as yours. You are constantly held captive by their web of Illusion, which is constructed in many different ways to make the Ego pleased to accept and dwell in that Illusion. All these ways are directed toward the five senses of the body, and beauty and happiness are always to be found in the fulfillment and gratification of the senses. The fascination of touch and feeling, the sight of form and color, the taste sensations of food and drink, as well as the hearing of sounds which stimulate the emotions associated with bodily experience, these have become of paramount importance and interest. The world of the senses is seen as the Third-dimension of Consciousness, whereas the Astral part of your experience is seen as the Fourth-dimension of Consciousness.

Instead of granting Light and empowerment to the Earth, you have enslaved your consciousness by turning your back on your Light. You have entered into agreement to destroy the ascension of the Earth's consciousness and create those conditions for its obliteration.

I have come to you at this time to awaken you to see your true destiny, before it is too late and the powers of darkness take your essence and Light with them. You, as well as they, will be cut off from the Light source of the star systems and will be absorbed into the eternal nothingness, to become once more prime matter for the Creator – Light; to await another time when the out-flow of consciousness will allow the opportunity for you to build a Light-body in the image of Light, and co-create forever in the Light of all that is –

I AM THAT I AM.([1])

This message will resume in three days. I suggest that next time you bring some recording equipment, so that my message will be given verbatim to the mass of Humanity for their salvation.'

The image faded and the capsule was mute and featureless as before. The afternoon light had returned to the room and the sun glared in through the dusty panes of the window. A hawk cried somewhere in the distant sky, its keening muffled somewhat by the hum of the air conditioner. There was a hot dry smell of sage. Rose looked elated but very tired, and Carl looked confused and equally exhausted. His face reflected conflicting emotions, which was unusual to see, because Carl rarely expressed any feelings. How deeply he had been touched by the message of the hologram I could not tell, but I was sure it had moved something in him.

Strange, strange and wonderful, I thought, and suddenly I realized how clear and open my mind had become. Everything washed through me – sharp sensations, sounds, smells, sights – like the sea through broken rock. The words of Zadore rang inside my hollow brain and no thought of mine intruded; but there was an echo from my heart – 'I AM that I AM. I AM that I AM!'

'Wow,' said Rose.

I looked at Rose, and she smiled. Her eyes had a light that seemed to flow right into me. My guts did a somersault – consciously I did not know why, but inwardly I felt it – we had shared something stupendous! There were no words but 'wow'.

Carl, on the other hand, had recovered his customary self, and was ready to talk. He started on about, 'What the heck was that all about?' and, 'Did you understand any of it?' to, 'Could somebody be playing a joke on us?' and so on, until I realized how exhausted I was as well. Too tired for questions and uninterested in intellectual explanations. Right then all I wanted to do was to go home, have a shower and a meal and crash. I could tell that Rose felt the same way. 'We're all washed out by this,' I said to Carl. 'Do you think we could let it go for a while? I need some time to think about what has happened.'

Carl shrugged. I guess he was glad to give rationalizing away because he did not even try to argue. Perhaps he felt as we did. 'I'll see you on Monday then,' he said. 'Just make sure you lock that thing up safely.'

CHAPTER 3

Second Transmission

On arriving Monday morning the first thing all of us wanted to do was get another look at the capsule. I guess the whole weekend long we had each been thinking about it. I know that for me it was a fascination that would not leave my consciousness alone. I must have spent all of my total waking hours dwelling on what the capsule's meaning was for me and for the world. I was even tempted to drive out to the site and take another peek but I fought that one because I knew that this miracle was not only mine – its message belonged to the others as well.

I had locked the capsule in the filing cabinet and we took it out not expecting anything immediate to happen. Indeed, I felt apprehensive and I'm sure the others did, remembering what pain it had caused us before. However, as soon as it was on the table the capsule commenced glowing and we all leaped back, with our hands ready to protect our eyes. Then I realized I had not set the tape machine, so risking blindness I ran and switched it on.

But this time no blinding light occurred. The hologram merely appeared, surrounded by its beautiful blue atmosphere, and the glowing image of Zadore spoke:

'There is no need to be afraid. After initially scanning your brain cells, the light beam from the capsule transferred information back to this computer, which allows my message to be conveyed in the language that you readily understand. I am not an alien from another planet. My home is the Sun of this solar system. I am Zadore, Keeper of the Solar Gate, and I have chosen this method of communication to bring to the enslaved and the suffering the means of breaking free from the Astral entities. Once you choose to receive the healing powers of the Galaxy, you can once more heal the Earth of the negative destruction that you have supported and still support. When this message is completed, the capsule will self destruct. Not immediately, but with sufficient time for you to return it to that place where you first discovered it.

A time wave is now affecting the consciousness of the planet and with it those who choose enlightenment for the planet and for themselves, and they will need to prepare to seek Light within their Being and fulfill their mission to give Light and Consciousness to the Earth.

Over the years the majority of individuals has not heeded the call of Light and has continued to live in a state of illusion. It is time for you to realize that you are not human beings, for their time in consciousness has not yet commenced. (2) You have been brainwashed into believing that you are human! You will learn that the Earth Children are yet to be born, for it is They who are to inherit the Earth, and this will only come to fruition after you have completed your commitment to integrate your higher dimensional Light and Consciousness for the Earth's ascension.

It is a time of decision, a decision as to whether you will now move your consciousness to the Earth-body you now inhabit, filling the Earth with greater Light, and allowing you to build a powerful Light Body of your own, or be reabsorbed into the total essence of Light, along with the perverse Astral Lords, and then to await another time when the out-flow of the breath of creation occurs again. If that is what you choose. You will then have no memory of past existence, but will become formative matter awaiting seeding to gain a light body which is one in the creative essence of all that is!

More will follow.'

The glowing ceased and the capsule was as before. My mind was in a whirl. Images of suns and lights and waves and bright beings spilled over themselves and over one another, and I barely knew what they were. I was in a state of wonder – like a child, and my thoughts hardly went beyond their primitive stage. And yet I did not mind being wordless – it did not seem to matter.

It was Carl who jerked me from my daze: 'So, the thing's a computer! And it scans brain cells! Why, with sophistication like that we could make a fortune on the open market. It would make every other computer obsolete!'

Aha, I thought. The voice of mercenary reason. I wondered if Carl had even listened to the rest of the transmission. Had he been too busy calculating heaven sent opportunities?

'As long as you can get Zadore to tell you how it's done,' put in Rose.

Startled, I stared at her. I had not thought she would react in the same way as Carl, but then I saw the look of disgust on her face and realized that I had missed the sarcasm in her tone.

And Carl did not notice, so caught up in his own world was he. 'Yes, that would be a problem, I suppose, at least at this early stage. But maybe, later on…'

Inwardly I groaned, yet I said nothing of what I felt. What could you say to someone in that state of mind that would not sound, to their ears, pompous and self righteous? Instead, I said:

'Well this is not getting our work done, and we have work to do. I suggest we get moving out to the trenches. After all we'll have plenty of time for contemplation over lunch. The way this morning is heating up I vote we break early, about eleven thirty, before it gets too hot. We can spend the rest of the day on reports and maybe have another go with the capsule. Okay?'

Rose nodded. 'Good idea. I don't fancy getting sunstroke for the sake of a few extra hours outside.

Besides I'm rather behind in my paperwork, it will be good to catch up.'

Carl agreed. Of course his reports were always up to date. He just wanted more time with the capsule; that was all, I am sure.

For the third time I measured the same layer of peat. Rose had given up altogether and was sitting on a rock, sipping thoughtfully at her water flask. Carl stood apart from us, staring into space.

The air around us sizzled with arid heat. You could almost hear the crackling and feel the electricity of thunderstorms that would never actually arrive but which threatened continuously. I found the atmosphere oppressive and was sick of the sweat making grimy rivers down my arms and hands. I looked at my watch…11.19am…near enough.

'Pack up time, okay?' I said to the others.

'OKAY!'

We trudged slowly back to the office, not saying much of anything to one another. Rose seemed rather more lively than either Carl or I and picked up the pace, drawing ahead.

'Ah, the energy of the young,' I said to Carl.

Without humor he stared at me, as if he resented me classifying him with myself, in the old codger category. Then, silently, he hurried after Rose, leaving me behind.

Reaching her, he began a subdued monologue, which I could not hear. I saw Rose nod a few times and say something, so I pushed myself to catch up with them. A disquiet regarding Carl was beginning to surface in my mind. I knew he was discussing the capsule with Rose and it really irritated me to think that he might be trying to exclude me from their considerations.

'What about a University?' Carl was saying.

'My Alma Mater might fund a research grant. That material the

17

capsule is made of sure would be interesting to them,' replied Rose.

'But it's a computer too, don't forget,' Carl went on eagerly. 'I still think the C.I.A. would pay—' He stopped abruptly when he realized I was right behind him.

'Pay for what, Carl?' I asked. 'The capsule or the information?'

Carl flushed. 'Well I hardly think the information....' he started to say, then, thinking better of it, continued, 'It's not much of an idea anyway. Forget I even mentioned it.'

I promised myself I would not forget it, but said nothing more. When we arrived at the office I let Carl have his way with the capsule. He was impatient to get started. However the capsule did not seem to be so eager.

Carl prodded it, tapped it, then gave it a whack, like you do to the TV when it won't work. 'God damned thing has probably broken down,' he said in a bitter voice.

'Maybe you have to say … please,' said Rose, grinning.

Carl scowled at her. But to me her tease made sudden sense. A flash in my consciousness told me that all that was required to activate the capsule was for us to sit quietly and focus our minds toward it. When I suggested we do so and the suggestion succeeded, both Rose and Carl looked very surprised.

The capsule glowed; the transmission commenced. I activated the recorder once more.

ZADORE SPOKE:

'What you have heard from my previous transmissions is that the consciousness which flows through your Earth bodies has been changed or manipulated into believing that the Illusion of the Third-dimension, as understood by the five senses, is the true reality of that, which you are. You now believe that you exist through this body consciousness and that you can control your destiny. You are continually told that you have free will, the choice to decide your fate. How can one imagine that one is free when one lives in an illusion? You do not have free will in your present state; you only have a choice to decide between the parameters contained in the Illusion, for the Illusion contains the morals and laws based on the definitive society in the country in which you live. He or she who may be seen as a good citizen in one country is looked at as being a criminal in another. Your freedom of choice, or will, applies to how you wish to behave and be seen by others who live with you in your illusion. You interpret your existence relative to your body and its senses, and how this relates to the world and the Universe. Your choices are based mainly on fears, and those fears relate to potential pain and suffering which your body may have to endure. This suffering and pain is seen as: death; poverty and sickness; war and destruction. Your freedom of will or purpose is bent by the frequencies of the Illusion of the Third-dimension, which binds you to body experiences.

To understand more, listen whilst the Earth speaks to you.'

The hologram changed and the image of Zadore was replaced by a glowing blue sphere.

THE EARTH SPEAKS:

'I am the expanding consciousness of the light and energy frequencies that radiate throughout the Universe, of which I am a part. This Universe is one of many Universes that exist in the creative being of Light. I am the child of the Sun. The Sun has many children that make up this solar system. Some of the Sun's children are now what you call dead planets, planets which have experienced the destructive powers of the Astral beings who continually work with the material of this solar system in the attempt to break free into the Galaxy, and gain greater power and control of the star systems.

Currently they are using the light frequencies of your entrapped consciousness to bring forth my destruction. They feel that through harnessing atomic power they will be able to use this to

19

thrust their consciousness beyond my radiation belts and free them to move deep into the Galaxy. They are constantly communicating with beings from other star systems, attempting an alliance to take control of the Galaxy itself.

I am a life form, a living organism that is constantly expanding in consciousness. That is, until your frequencies came and were enslaved by the Astral beings. Up until then my destiny was controlled solely by the Sun. It was time to prepare for my ascension, and the Galactic consciousness decided that greater light must be beamed through the Sun from other star systems, to assist my growth. My growth of consciousness is predetermined and precise, and I am still guided by the love of my Mother Sun, as well as the other stars in the Galaxy. In my own time and space, I will be a self conscious, self luminous being like Mother Sun, and in this ever expanding and ever creating Universe, I, too, will produce the patterns for conscious beings from my own nature. My progress has been steady and expansive, through the love and energies flowing to me from the Galaxy.

Unfortunately, some 30,000 years ago some of the early beings who came here to seed my organism used their growing powers to enter my morphogenetic fields and alter their functions. They built stone structures to contact other star systems and encode these other energies into my fields in an attempt to increase their power base within the Galaxy.(3) When this failed, it was time for your Light frequencies to seed the bodies which I have evolved for my own conscious enlightenment.

Initially my consciousness began to expand, and I began to increase my Light. Gradually, those previous forms, the Astral beings, began to weave their evil web to create the Illusion that was to enslave your consciousness, and, in time, you forgot your purpose. You were then dual beings with a dual consciousness, and the consciousness of the Third-dimension made you fall asleep to your higher consciousness and purpose. I will speak further on this, however first we must go back in time, to the time of my birth, and for this my Mother Sun will speak.'

Now the light of the Earth was eclipsed by the brilliant corona of the Sun. Its light softened as its message entered our consciousness.

THE SUN SPEAKS

'There is much to be understood by entities such as you who are currently transmitting your consciousness to Human, or Earth bodies. After you have received all the transmissions from the Keeper of the Solar Gate, you will understand your purpose and why you must turn away from your enslavement in order to fulfill your mission. You have already learnt that you have strayed from that mission and, as such, have caused innumerable tensions to the consciousness of my Earth Child. Soon you will enter a time zone of the planetary decision and it is important for your own salvation to make the choice of your direction. This message is to awaken those of the planet to focus their consciousness back to their original source through ME. Soon, through my rays, an energy vortex will be focused to the Earth, which will direct you to the healing of your consciousness so that you will turn your Ego away from the Illusion back to the Light of your own true self and, in so doing, produce an enlightenment for my child-planet.

It is necessary for you to understand how my child-planet was born. The Earth is a part of my Light Essence, which was an extension of my Being. This essence moved away from my body in a spiral curve rotating in a clockwise motion. I have had several children; one in particular was named Mars by you. I mention Mars because it has reached a fate of bareness and death that I do not want to see happen to Earth. The Earth is now suffering many onslaughts to its integrity and consciousness, by both you and the Astrals, that parallels the destruction of Mars. I am determined that the fate of Earth will not be the same as that of Mars.

As this brilliant ball of light moved away from me, like a

21

projectile moving in a clockwise motion, the further it moved from me the slower its speed became, until it reached a point of inertia and became motionless. Then, due to the force of attraction, it began to reverse its rotation, moving in a counter-clockwise spin. To the human mind this seems of little importance, however the rotatory spin of energy determines that, which your current science calls polarity. Most are aware that polarity is referred to as positive and negative energies and the determination of which is positive or negative is dependent on the directional spin of the electrons of which it is composed. This directional spin then determines that, which is called polarity. Thus a counter-clockwise spinning electron has a positive polarity and a clockwise spinning electron a negative polarity. My Being always moves in a clockwise motion, and when I birthed the Earth it too moved through the ethers in a clockwise motion. When it reached that point of inertia and began a counter-clockwise spin, it changed its polarity. The altered polarity of the Earth made it the opposite to that of mine. Instead of being fiery, it became hardened matter.

Such a reversal of energy caused a cooling effect, hardening the surface of the planet. As the light hardened, it became crystalline and solidified. This planet child of mine has been and still is nurtured by my radiance and the forces of consciousness that flow through me, to assist its growth and ascension that it shall eventually become a brilliant star and, in turn, promote greater consciousness throughout the Universe.'

THE EARTH RETURNS:

'**B**efore I began my counter-clockwise movement, I was still exhibiting the radiant energy of my Mother Sun. At this stage of my birth I shared the Light and Consciousness of my Mother. Once I reversed my polarity, I began my own evolution. I developed my own frequency and ascension in consciousness. Prior to this my being was composed solely of the energies of my Mother, however once I began my own frequency, my polarity altered and these current frequencies are the opposite to those which previously formed my being. Such a transformation created energy reactions between my Mother Sun and myself, in that I could then react with the Sun, to energize and grow.

Surrounding my being are two radiation belts. The closest of these two belts is located between 2,000 and 5,000 kilometers from my surface, and the second belt is located from 13,000 to 19,000 kilometers from my surface. Prior to the change of my axis spin, both these belts were very close to my surface, and they are composed of energies which are of the same frequency as that of the Sun. Once I began my counter-clockwise motion, these radiation belts were pushed away from my surface to their present positions. This push was caused by my polarity reversal, and subsequently a cooling effect occurred on my surface.

In terms of human time my growth and development may seem long and enduring. For me, it is a period of excitement and learning. Like any child, I drew great pleasure from all the knowledge that my mother Sun imparted to me. As the polarity of my body became more crystalline, and reflected my Mother's Light, my radiation belts began to absorb those patterns beamed from Mother Sun. As this is maintained, my continuous growth in consciousness is ensured. These patterns have now been called by those of you who have come to recognize them, morphogenetic patterns or L-fields, (Life-fields).

As my body cooled, gases formed and rose up above my surface and outward into the atmosphere created by the radiation belts. This upward movement caused the gases to become more dense, and they then precipitated moisture back to the surface of my body. As these cool waters touched my still hot surface, they turned into steam, and were drawn back into the atmosphere by the Sun's warm rays. For aeons, my atmosphere was covered by warm mist, and also heavy rain constantly fell, which gradually caused a cooling effect, cutting crevices on my surface, where it lay, forming oceans.

The cooling caused by my altered polarity trapped much of my Mother's original energies below my surface mantle. In those areas where the crust was thin, my Mother's energies burst through the surface, throwing molten lava and gases into the atmosphere, creating changes to the atmosphere.

Eventually a stage was reached in my development when my Mother began to weave her magic. The morphogenetic, or L-fields, are those basic patterns which were embedded in my radiation belts for my ascension in consciousness. It was only after the waters covered my hard body that these fields could be transferred to my consciousness. The morphogenetic patterns, which are responsible for all form that exists on my surface, were reflected by the Sun through the radiation belts where they were embedded. My watery surface was able to capture the reflected energy patterns where they took form. The first patterns were simple bacteria, which were transformed by the photosynthesis of the Sun. This caused many gases to emit oxygen. As the oxygenation process continued in the salty waters, simple cellular organisms formed to the corresponding pattern found in the radiation belts. Over a period of time my watery body was filled with all manner of plant and animal life. The next step was the metamorphosis of the sea organisms to the land. There was a gradual movement from the sea, as the organisms began their adaptation to a drier environment.

Modern man, and more especially those of scientific persuasion, view my Nature as being an experiment in the evolution of the Universe, that life forms are trialed and then rejected. They see those evolutionary changes to my consciousness as meaningless attempts to produce life forms, and not in accord with their perceptions, for they feel that they hold all the consciousness of the Universe and that I am merely an inert mass. They do not see that the dinosaurs were a step in the evolving nerve tissue, to carry greater levels of frequency. Also their bodies supplied nutrients back into my soils for further creativity and the evolution of modified forms through the ever increasing patterns transmitted by Mother Sun through the radiation belts.

Gradually, I was able to produce more intense and sophisticated bodies or organisms that could capture greater amounts of consciousness from the Sun. All the birds, animals, insects, fish and human type organisms were developed, and are still developing, to be used as antennae to receive light frequencies from the Galaxy.

More will follow.'

The transmission was over. I felt worn out, as much by the amount of information I had received as by the excessive heat of the day. There was almost too much to think about in this transmission, yet I knew it was vital to do so.

What was the reality of those Control Beings, or Astral Lords, as Zadore had called them? How really trapped were we? What was the meaning of our breaking free from illusion? And what would it mean for us and for the life and environment of this planet if and when we did so?

And how beautiful was the story of the Sun and Earth. Yet it blew my scientist's mind with its evolutionary concepts.

But most incredible of all, were we truly such wonderful Beings of Light, albeit controlled and stifled, as the message suggested? Contrary to all I had been taught, I began to feel that it was so, and the feeling seemed to free my spirit from all the oppression and guilt it had ever known. Perhaps Rose and Carl were equally impressed, and equally needing to digest the mass of information, for neither of them appeared keen for much discussion.

In fact we all decided that we'd had enough for one day and wanted to go our separate ways.

I switched off the tape recorder, leaving the tape in it for the next session. I locked everything in the filing cabinet. Carl was watching me intently and his manner was disturbing. A worry niggled somewhere, but I was to shrug it off as I drove back home to LA. Only later would I learn not to underestimate the value of niggling intuition.

CHAPTER 4

Imprisoned Light

That night I had great difficulty in sleeping. I seemed to be plagued by meaningless dreams about the Earth and Sun, as they formed grotesque figures. Then the Earth hologram came clear, and spoke to me: 'This capsule is all a trick. It was planted during the Cold War by the old Soviet regime as a plot to undermine the U.S. Tomorrow you must take it away and bury it in the desert where it cannot be found, in an old mine shaft.'

This was followed by the form and face of my mother, who has been dead for several years now:

'Take heed, Jon, of what you have just heard, for to follow this current path will only lead to danger!'

My body began to ache and my head throbbed as I awoke in a sweat. I sat up in bed with a strong feeling that what I had just experienced was not right. I have remembered enough dreams over the years to be able to recognize what was a simple dream and what constituted an invasion of my psychic state. After some time I calmed myself down and eventually went to sleep.

About 2.00am I felt my return to a border state of consciousness, and before me appeared Zadore, as brilliantly as in the hologram. This Being radiated light and peace, so that I was not afraid. I heard Zadore speak to my consciousness:

'Jon, you have been selected to carry my message to the world. There are many forces at work that want to prevent this happening. You have already this night experienced some of the methods by which those forces will attempt to manipulate your consciousness through dream states. I will teach you how to prevent any further intrusion; however you will also need to maintain awareness during the day. I must warn you also about Carl. He covets the capsule and tapes, and it is his intention to sell the information to the government intelligence agency, or any other group who will satisfy his need for wealth. Such people and agencies will only suppress the information, as they have done to other information in the past. Tomorrow morning go to the site office early and make copies of the existing tapes, and keep your silence regarding their existence. I am depending on you to be the one who is to carry this message to those in the world who are waiting for the change. In the future I will direct you to those who will work with you in having the message distributed. Sleep now and remember what I have just told you.'

On waking at 6.00A.M., I felt refreshed and invigorated. This was rather surprising, I thought, considering what I had been through during the night. I felt within myself that I must heed the warnings of Zadore, and quickly got ready to go to the site before the others would arrive.

On the way I stopped by a Mart for some extra tapes, as I did not want anyone to notice that the store in the office cupboard was diminishing rather more rapidly than it ought. Once at the office I made my copies on Hi-Speed Dub, then hid them away in my bag. I realized I would have to do this as a matter of course from now on. I made sure I returned the originals to the filing cabinet and secured it. If Carl was to be a problem, as Zadore warned, then keeping the cabinet locked except when we needed something from it was the only option. And the key must remain with me, on my own chain.

Only after I had completed all this did I give myself a breather and a cup of coffee, and reflect on the unquestioning way I had reacted to the dream of Zadore. Of course I had not seen the experience as a dream; otherwise I might have been less urgent in my actions. No, it had not been a dream, but how had Zadore entered my consciousness without the capsule? And more disturbing still, that other 'dream' – what did it portend?

First to arrive, some fifteen minutes later, was Carl, carrying his camera. He went straight to the cabinet.

'Hey, where is the key?'

'I'm hanging on to it,' I said. 'Just to be sure everything is kept safe.'

Carl looked peeved. 'What? Don't you trust Rose or me?'

I lied. 'No, it's not that. It's just that I think one of us should take charge of it rather than our just leaving it in the desk drawer when we're not here. You never know who could break in and find it.'

Carl shrugged. His face revealed that he did not believe me, but all he said was, 'Well, can I have it now? I thought of collecting some photographic evidence – of the capsule as it is – and when the transmission is taking place. Okay?'

I was not very keen on that idea. But how could I object? Carl would become either belligerent or suspicious, or both, if I did.

'Okay … fine. Here it is.'

When Rose eventually arrived, a little late, Carl began talking to her about the tapes, and it was obvious to me that he was looking to her for an ally in his need to secure everything for his own use. Rose, however, was non committal, and I think this annoyed him, for sulkily he took the capsule and recorder and sat down alone in front of the table, intending to concentrate on activating the hologram all by himself. Rose gave me a look which asked: 'Have you two been fighting, or what?' then she stood watching Carl.

After a few moments and no success Carl grew very red in the face and angry. Always the compassionate one, Rose dismissed his sulks and went to help him. She cast me a pleading glance, but stubbornly I refused to join them. Let them try, I thought unkindly. After what Zadore had told me I was sure it would not do any good, not for Carl anyway.

I was right. Nothing happened. In frustration they both got up and went to make some coffee. I was still feeling rather ungenerous so I took my place at the table and after gazing for a moment at the capsule, I asked it mentally to begin transmission.

Immediately it commenced glowing, so I switched on the recorder and announced the Third Transmission.

My sense of triumph was dimmed rather by a prickle of conscience regarding my behavior, and by Rose's reaction to my success.

'Well I'll be.... So you're the only one who gets it going!' she exclaimed from her coffee cup. There was no resentment or envy in her tone, only surprise and wonder, and she hurried right over.

Not so Carl, however. He would not sit down, although he acted as if nothing mattered and flourished his camera theatrically. Yet from behind that camera lens he glared at me. The resentment was all too plain to me, and a reason for worry, perhaps.

But I could not concern myself with Carl's antics – the transmission had started and it was the Earth which spoke first:

THE EARTH SPEAKS:

'At the conclusion of the last Transmission I stated that the Sun had placed morphogenetic patterns in the radiation belts that surround my body in order that I could produce organisms that would act as antennae, so that I could attract those frequencies that would enlarge my consciousness. It is now time to explain to you what was my next transformation, and this will be told to you by the Sun.'

30

THE SUN SPEAKS:

'You have now heard that the conscious growth of my Earth-child was dependent on the continual radiations that I beamed to it, as well as the morphogenetic patterns in the radiation belts. How this has been understood by the consciousness of the Earth beings was written in a simple language in the book of Genesis, where it referred to how God created the Earth, its plant and animal life. This then is the simple story of my seeding the radiation belts with the patterns which the Earth could use for its own evolution.

Many individuals dwelling on the Earth and experiencing life only through information gained by their five senses, feel that all of the mysteries of the Universe can be solved in an intellectual way. Because they think that intellectual understanding represents the peak of human experience and knowledge, their achievements are limited. It is impossible for consciousness grounded in the sensual Illusion of the Third-dimension to penetrate the deeper mysteries that belong to the higher dimensions. Mankind is kept in perpetual ignorance by the Astral Lords, who continually keep the consciousness of the race focused on the area of intellectual power.

My message is important for beings like you who are trapped in this plane of egoistic consciousness. I will now reveal to you some of the creative frequencies that underlie my relationship with Earth, and how this affects your continual presence on this planet, even though you have forgotten your purpose for being here.

From my essence I continually radiate my energies, which are flowing throughout the ethers of the Universe. These grounded radiations that have been recognized by you as ions are minute packets of energy that I radiate both to the Earth and the other planets in the Solar System. They also form the radiation belts of the Earth, and are of the original essence of the Earth when it moved from my body.

31

I am able to use these powered energy packets to convey to the Solar System many frequencies that are necessary for growth and consciousness. Beyond my own being, I too receive frequencies from the Galactic essence Itself, some of which are necessary for the growth and consciousness of my own Solar System.

The ions carry to the planet the frequency that has been termed by you as Life Force, and which is actually the energy frequency of the Universe which produces consciousness on a biological level.

This Life Energy is of an opposite polarity to the ions which act as its carrier through space. It flows with the ions passing out of my body to the morphogenetic fields in the radiation belts.

Actually, these frequencies do not flow, rather they move in a spiral fashion. Along with the Life Energy, other frequencies ride with the ions. These consist of those elemental forms of consciousness which have been loosely termed little people, fairies, devas etc. They have a deep understanding of the morphogenetic patterns and they constantly pass into the Third-dimension throughout the whole Universe. They move through my consciousness to the Earth, and their purpose is to constantly maintain the forms that are generated through the morphogenetic fields. You are not aware of the tremendous frustration that you are causing to these workers through all your meddling in the structure and functions of the varying formations and organisms on the Earth. Their transmission is of a continual nature, as they assist in the maintenance of the expression of all the forms which are built by the Earth as it ascends in consciousness. It is time that you appreciate that these elemental beings are responsible for the growth and care of the bodies that you project your consciousness into. If you only realized and felt their presence in your aura, you would then know that you should ascribe all healing of bodily ills to them and not fuss about with experimenters who are still playing with life energies.

The mass of human consciousness negates the existence of elemental consciousness and continues to push the body into a polluted toxic mess of disease, shutting out the healing and beauty of the organism.

You, too, are light frequencies that spiral through my being from many Star Systems in the Galaxy. Your consciousness travels with the Life Energy through the radiation belts, where you attach to those karmic patterns that you have created individually and collectively over millennia through your forgetfulness of your true purpose and origins.

It is now time for me to reveal to you how you allowed your consciousness to be captured by those Astral Lords who dwell on the Fourth-dimension.

Many of you who are suffering in your own created prison, dwell both in the Third and Fourth- dimensions continually, although you are unaware of it, or are reluctant to speak of it for fear of being locked in a mental institution. Generally you feel that you are in control of your life as you function in the Third-dimension, and that is because you accept that it is the ONLY dimension of existence. Often, when consuming an excess of drugs or alcohol or when in a dream state, you become conscious of the Fourth-dimension reality. The daily cycle of darkness, or night, that envelopes half of the Earth, produces old, instinctive fears, which often allow invasion of your consciousness and body by nefarious beings of Fourth, or Astral, dimension. The following day, when my light illumines your habitation, those experiences in the darkness are quickly pushed into your unconscious as being figments your imagination, to be ignored and forgotten.

In your darkened consciousness you are not able to easily comprehend that, which I am projecting to you. What you must understand, now and forever, is that YOU do not actually exist on the Earth and are not that body which you feel is YOU. You do not exist on the Astral dimension either. However you are constantly experiencing certain frequencies of both dimensions as you project your consciousness through my being. YOU ARE light frequencies that are being projected through me from throughout the whole Galaxy. You are doing this, for it is the only way that you can build a Light Body or Soul Body. Your quest for evolution has been abruptly stopped due to your agreement with the Astral Lords to attempt to control the Earth and bend it to your collective purpose, although you have no purpose, you are but slaves to the purposes of the Astrals themselves.(4)

You will only awaken by effort and knowledge. The morphogenetic patterns are those patterns which initially clothe you in the essence of matter. Now you receive your initial form on the Fourth- dimension and then pass through the second radiation belt, which clothes the consciousness in a more dense fabric, which is called the 'etheric' body. The radiation belts act as step-down transformers, to move your projected consciousness into being able to express itself in these dense frequencies. These condensers are literally termed chakras. The finer chakras are found on your Fourth-dimensional form, relative to the first radiation belt, and the more dense etheric chakras are patterned in the second radiation belt. When the etheric form matches the body form produced by the Earth, your consciousness can spiral through all the levels of the two dimensions and manifest in a sensual body. The Earth-body channels the consciousness through a system of endocrine glands, which are grounding the energies of the etheric form.

Now you have arrived, and, through the Ego which exists on the highest level of the Third- dimension in the etheric band, you begin to experience yourself as a separate unit of consciousness clothed and restricted in matter. This is as it was meant to be. However, once you began to experience the inexplicable ecstasy and joy of sensuality, you became obsessed by its attraction, and began to forget. It is absolutely necessary for you to experience this dimensional sensuality, for it was that, which Light was to also experience through you. You were encouraged by the Astral Lords to explore greater depths of sensuality, drawing your consciousness deeper into the dense fabric of matter. In your joy of feeling free to be an individual entity, they invited you to join with them in ruling all that you could see with your eyes, and they promised that you would achieve greater power as you conquered this Third-dimension.

And so you fell into matter, and forgot your true light, which is continually spiraling through me.

Because the Astrals have mastered the energies of both the Third and Fourth-dimensions, they easily hold power over you and all your actions. For those who have desired to become as powerful as the Astrals, they virtually have sold their souls to the Devil, for they now cannot build a Light Body. The Astral Lords see that their return to greater power can be assisted by using others' light energies and directing them to their use. If they could destroy the Earth, they would disrupt the radiation belts, allowing them an exit from the Fourth-dimension.

The radiation belts were sealed by the Lords of Karma – those beings who are also termed Time Lords. They impose restrictions on exit from the Fourth-dimension of all beings who have not formed their Light Body and fulfilled their obligations to the Earth's conscious evolvement. By denying your birthright and seeking power in the two dimensions, and by believing that your Ego consciousness is greater than your Light consciousness, this leads you to destructive actions to others of your kind, to your own self image, and binds you to these two dimensions, requiring continual return until you awaken to your true self.(5) Wanting to maintain control of your Light Essence, the Astral Lords have convinced you that it is essential for you to return to evolve your Light Body. By keeping you from discovering the simple way of accomplishing this, they have kept you locked in an endless loop of return. It is time that you awaken from this subterfuge. These transmissions will enlighten your consciousness and allow you to free yourself from your self imposed prison. You only need to WANT to!

This concludes today's transmission. Zadore will, in further transmissions, teach you about the Astral Lords, their controls, and what you must do to diminish their power over you.'

A heavy silence hung in the room after that third recording. We had never discussed the content of the transmissions. The affair of the capsule was so new and so staggering that I believe it had shaken us all off balance into a state where our thinking was unclear and somewhat confused.

For myself, I knew that the ideas presented had my brain in a whirl. Such beautiful concepts – so vast and terrifying – they moved in me some very primal feelings, which, now I came to face them, seemed to have been with me all my life. I was not at the stage of dissecting the information, yet I thought I would soon have to. In spite of my positive feeling for the message of the amazing hologram, a part of me wanted to question it. And challenge its assertions. Upbringing and social conditioning can be very powerful forces, but none are so powerful as the force of Reason. It is Reason which rules our world in its tightfisted, lop-sided way. Alone, Reason deduces the Universe from such evidence as the five senses provide, casts its parts in concrete and labels them pedantically. Alone, it dislikes mystery, beauty or wonder, and will pour scorn on any other vision of the world.

We ought to talk, I thought. We can't just sit here.

I looked at Rose. Her eyes were closed and her face had an inward expression. A cloud of light seemed to surround her strong, attractive features. Could she be meditating? I did not like to disturb her if she was.

So I glanced at Carl who had put down his camera and was seated next to Rose. I was surprised to see that his thin, sallow face was contorted and agonized looking. It appeared that he was fighting a fierce inner battle, which no one else could share. He reminded me of the image in the painting 'The Cry', by Munch; I could almost hear him screaming out his cry for help. But help for what?

Gingerly, I approached him. 'Carl, are you okay?'

A dumb question, I know, when it was so obvious that he wasn't. But I had to say something.

'Has the message affected you? I know it has done so to me. Did it give you any feelings or memories? I certainly had a few,' I said in a calm, reasonable voice.

Rose had come awake. I saw the shock in her eyes when she observed Carl.

'Me too,' she said, with equal care. 'Carl, you look so unhappy. I found the message so uplifting.

What's wrong?'

Seeming to recover and ceasing his twisting, Carl glared at both of us.

'What would you two know about life? I suppose you think you know it all! There's much more to life than digging the ground and dating earthquakes. Life is an endless parade of trials. Life is hell!' he blurted out.

We were taken aback by the vehemence of his feeling, as much as by the words, but, gamely, Rose said:

'That's pretty heavy, Carl. Why are you so bitter?'

'Bitter! You don't know the meaning of the word. What I know about this life is nothing that this damned capsule can tell.'

I didn't like the way this exchange was going; nevertheless I said, 'Well, what more do you know that is so terrible? I thought we were hearing it all.'

'You wouldn't want to know, and you would never understand,' Carl growled.

With that he seemed to metamorphose, and we stared into the eyes of a tortured, possessed being. It was a human soul in Hell and it was a sight I never want to see again. Poor Carl, I thought he was going to have a seizure. His body twitched and shook uncontrollably, and all the while you could tell that he as locked in a massive battle with some nefarious force, while he struggled valiantly to break free.

It was frightening. Rose was nearly in tears and I felt ill myself. 'Oh God, do something to help him,' Rose begged.

'I don't know what to do!' I said helplessly.

Then, abruptly from Carl's twisted face came a terrible howl like that of a wild wolf. The hairs prickled on my neck.

'Oh, God,' moaned Rose, as Carl slumped in his chair, as if he had collapsed. She stood up and leaned toward him.

Without any thought the words sprang from my mouth, 'Don't touch him!' and Rose recoiled, sinking back into her chair.

I moved over to Carl. I saw tears starting down his cheeks. I touched his hand and said: 'Carl, we're old friends, don't despair, we're old friends. What's the problem?'

Carl's body shook uncontrollably, as the tears welled up within him, and he sobbed continually. Thankfully he seemed to be breaking free from his possession.

After a couple of minutes he began to regain his composure. He then quietly and without pause related to us the story of his life experience.

It was a story that shocked and horrified both Rose and myself. It almost managed to overwhelm Rose completely, and she sat all the while with her head lowered, in her own battle of emotion. I listened in grief as Carl told a tale of something so monstrous I did not want to believe it.

And yet I must. This story is not a fantasy, nor is it the raving of an insane mind, although it is a wonder that its events had not driven Carl hopelessly mad by then. It is a story I should hope would never be repeated on this planet, however I fear that its horror might not be exclusive to Carl. In some ways the wars, the plagues, and the bloody terrors experienced by many souls in our modern times are no less terrifying and destructive. In some ways many are living in the same hell as Carl. Yet of all

the stories Carl's is the worst – the most barbarous and brutal and inhuman I have ever heard.

CHAPTER 5

The Dark Side

CARL'S STORY

'I was only two years old when my family moved from Germany to San Francisco. In those early years my father appeared to always radiate an air of detachment, for he never expressed any signs of emotion or love. I always tried to be close to him, but this was not to be. My mother likewise was cold and efficient. She always looked after the house and my needs, but never seemed to give me the love or help I longed for. Later I put this down in part to the hardships my parents experienced in Germany during the war; however I found out that this was not the case.

'The family came from Rostock, in East Germany. My father was not a young man when I was born, he was forty five years old. He never spoke about the war, or what he did during that time. I don't think that he was in uniform, and I never saw him wear anything other than a black suit when he went out, and even at home. There were never any photographs in the house and, unlike most families, no photographs of when he was a child.

'Our house was not far from Fisherman's Wharf. It was one of those two storey wooden homes on the hill looking across to Alcatraz. The old house does not exist there now as it was destroyed by an earthquake, and was replaced by a brick building with underground car spaces, which more than likely will not survive a serious shake, as it is weaker than the original building.

'Upstairs in the old house was a third floor, or more correctly a dormer. The door to the dormer was always locked. My room was just below the dormer, and often in those early years I was disturbed during the night by voices and by sounds of something hitting the floor.

'One night, not long after my seventh birthday, I was awakened by the voices of my mother and father downstairs. They seemed to be talking louder than usual, or at least my mother was. I thought that they were having an argument. They were speaking in German, which was the language at home. I got out of my bed and went out to the top of the stairs where I could see the light streaming out of the partly open living room door. My mother was talking, and I listened:

"'No,' she said. 'You cannot do that, you cannot involve the boy. He is only seven. What future will he have after you do this?"

'My father replied in his usual quiet monotone. He never expressed any emotion, not even anger. However his words were menacing:

"'There is nothing else to be said. I must give the boy; that is the agreement. If not they will call in my debt. I have made with them this pact and it will be my own release. That is my conditional agreement with them."

"'Hah! You and your conditions! Where has it ever got you? Even in this country you are not free, and you think that the sacrifice of my son will give you the power you seek for eternity!"

"'Enough! You do not know it all. Hitler is dead, and what I did then was solely for those who rule this planet, and I have been guaranteed a place in this ruling elite, and I will have it. The spirit of Hitler will return to this planet within the next twelve months, however he is expendable now, as are all other puppets the Lords create and use."

"'Then why involve the boy? There will be no escape for him either; he will be damned for eternity."

"'Be silent! Your understanding is limited to this dimension. You joined me to produce the vehicle that was acceptable to the Lords, and you too agreed as such. You cannot stop that, which has been decreed. There is no more to be said."

'Whatever they were talking about made no sense to me, except that it involved me. Then I heard

my father's chair push back, and I quickly ran back to my room and jumped into bed. I feigned sleep as I heard his footsteps climb the stairs. I knew he was coming to my room, and I was scared of what may happen.

'The door opened slowly and I saw his silhouette in the doorway. I am sure he did not know that I was awake. From the door he whispered: "Carl, soon you will be returning to your home, and I will be there to guide you."

'I felt a shiver go up my spine, and a cold feeling of fear swept through my consciousness. I felt like screaming out in terror, but nothing came out. I watched his figure standing in the half light. It seemed to grow larger, and expand to fill the doorway, like a giant bat. He then turned and closed the door.

'At that time I thought that this was the worst night of my life. But this would soon be eclipsed by another. During the night I had continual nightmares and they all involved my father. His form floated through my consciousness. At times he smiled that cold, expressionless smile that gave no sense of comfort, and then his face turned into that of a wolf with glaring eyes and foaming mouth and white fangs that bit me on the throat. My blood spurted out and I screamed in terror. The wolf became a black bat that flew at me and sucked up the blood coming from my wound. This seemed endless throughout the night, and only just before dawn did I fall into a heavy dreamless sleep.

'The next morning I awoke with the warm sun streaming through my window. It was mid Fall, about early October, and the sun still had some of the summer warmth. I could hear the streetcars grinding their way up the hill from the wharves, and felt a little more reassured. Then my mother appeared in the doorway.

'"Hurry up, sleepy head, or you will be late for school."

'After that night I began to live in fear of both my mother and father. In my child mind I sensed that I was in danger. I knew that I was not really a child, but that in this small body I was vulnerable. I didn't know where to turn to and had nowhere to run. We had no relatives, and my folks had no close friendships. My father taught German at the High School, but did not mix with the faculty. My mother always took me to school each day, and she did not get involved with other mothers. The kids at school seemed to constantly taunt me, as Germans were not the most popular citizens in the late forties.

'The next few weeks passed quickly and the events of that night began to fade in my child mind. On November 1st – All Saints Day – things came to a head and all my fears exploded. The day before, other kids in the neighborhood had walked the streets for Halloween. I was not involved in the celebration as it was not our custom. It seemed to me a lively day for the other kids, and I longed to go out and 'trick or treat'. However that day passed and by supper of the next evening I felt there was a strong tension between my father and mother, and instinctively I knew it involved me. I became muddled and confused, and felt apprehensive.

'When we finished supper, my father said that I was to accompany him to the dormer room, that as I was seven it was time for me to begin my life's purpose. I looked at my mother for some reassurance. She stared with that expression that seemed to look straight through me. She said not one word.

'I was feeling tired and scared, and it was late. My father left the room and about ten minutes later he returned. I was taken aback by his appearance. He was dressed in a long black robe

42

tied at the waist with a belt which was covered with strange metal symbols. On the left side of the gown near the heart was a white circle with a black swastika. Around his neck was a chain with a cross attached, however the cross was hanging upside down, otherwise it was a normal crucifix. His eyes glowed like black coals, as if in anticipation of some great event that was for him and not me.

'I looked at my mother and it seemed that she was in a trance, she sat motionless. I felt that she cared, and wanted her to speak to me.

'"Mother," I said.

There was no reply, only a flicker in her eyes conveyed that she was aware, and possibly afraid of my father.

'"Come," said my father. This time there was a slight anger at my hesitation. 'We ascended the stairs and he stopped at the door of my room.

'"Carl," he ordered, 'take off all your clothes and leave them here."

'Shivering, I obeyed. The November air was quite cold. and this part of the house had no heating. We must have looked a strange couple, the tall black figure and a small, white, naked child moving silently up the staircase, lit only by the light of a solitary candle held high in my father's hand.'

Carl began to shake continuously. It appeared that he might not be able to go on with the story. I was about to offer him a glass of water when he pulled himself together and continued:

'At the door my father took a large key from the pocket of his gown and opened the door. A rush of stale, moldy, damp air filled my nostrils as we entered the room. He gently closed the door behind him. I was pleased that he did not lock it, for I might

43

want to run away, but I couldn't see where I could run to.

'I stood by the entrance as he lit a large candle on the left side of the room, and a similar one on the other side. The soft illumination from the candles revealed a strange world. In the flickering light I saw a reading stand with what appeared to be an ancient book, which was open. The pages seemed to have strange diagrams on them, which meant nothing to me. Between the candles there was a square painted on the floor. Inside this square were three circles. At the corners of the square were five-pointed stars or pentacles, and between each of the circles were more strange symbols; some were similar to those on the belt my father wore.

'In front of the large square was another circle which had a triangle inside it; the point was facing away from the square. The walls of the room had various symbols, but the only one that I could recognize was the swastika.

'My father pushed back his cowl, revealing an expression glowing with anticipation. "'Now," he said aloud. "It's time, time for my freedom and ascension to power!"

'A cold shiver moved up my spine and I knew that all was not well, especially for me.

'He took my hand and led me to the central circle in the large square. He did not let go of my hand, it was as if I was chained to the being in black. He had never explained to me why this was to be or what I was expected to do. It was my initiation; he only said when I questioned him.

'My father looked at me. "Do not move from my side unless I indicate. Do you understand?" 'Frightened, I only nodded.

'Then my father began, in a voice so strange, to speak most peculiarly. Or so to my inexperienced ears. In my short life I had not been exposed to religious ceremony and had never heard chanting before. But this was what it was. Yet it was the chant of a ritual such as that never seen in a place of Christian worship, or any good-intentioned heathen one either. It was the chant of the Damned, and, for some cruel reason, every word of it was impressed on my memory forever.

'In some strange and awful way it is the one speech I have

remembered in full when quite easily I have forgotten many others. But why have I remembered it? Why, oh why, does it have to torment me all my life?'

Carl faltered again and the shaking returned. But only for a moment.

'My father spoke the chant in German, which I still understand fluently,' he said in a flat, matter of fact way. 'I will therefore have to translate for you.'

His thin tortured face raised to the ceiling, his eyes rolled backward, and then – and I shall never forget this – in a morbid voice that was not his own he chanted:

'"Omnipotent and Eternal Spirit of all the powers of this and the darker worlds, I Razparil, beseech that thou would'st send my spirit, Astaroth, of the Order of Baal, whom thou hast appointed as Master of the inner worlds that provide the power to the bearers of the Astral Realm, that my power and service to you will continue until eternity. Astaroth has been my servant under the pact that was signed in blood in the winter of 1934, when we agreed that I would provide the services of the Masters of these realms to the War Lord Hitler, so that thy purposes for the future of this planet will be done.

'"Spirits, whose assistance I require, behold this sign!" 'My father held up in his left hand the inverted crucifix.

'"Obey the power of this sign, and our sacred pentacle, come out of your hidden caves and darkened places, cease your torment on those unhappy mortals, come and know our demands. We command you by the Mysterious Names X…X…X…X…'(6)

'"I conjure thee, that you attend to the words of my mouth, that thou come forthwith, readily show thyself that we may see you, and audibly hear you, speak to us and fulfill our desires.'"

The chant had ended. Carl's head dropped forward, his eyes refocused, although to me they still looked glazed. His voice was normal again, though it trembled:

'A furious wind rushed through the atmosphere of the room, causing the candles to flicker, and before us, in the center of the triangle in the opposite circle, a grotesque figure manifested. It was no taller than me, but was gross and heavy. Its head was human-like with a dark beard, and teeth that were pointed like a dog's. Its eyes were red and smoldering, like the eyes that had appeared in my dream. Instead of hands it had claws that moved like fingers. Its eyes glared out towards us and with a rasping sounding voice, it spoke!

'"Razparil, you have called forth Astaroth, messenger of the great King Belial. It is now time for us to complete our pact, and for you to be raised to an Astral Lord, one who will forthwith work directly under Belial. You were given the power and authority to create and fulfill the desire for power and evil in those who seek it. It was recorded that you moved those frequencies through the one called Adolf Hitler and set forth that reign of fear and terror on this planet. So much so that he referred to you as the superman of extreme cruelty. At that time you had perfected the art of influence of the human mind in dream states, and this is one of the major requirements of Astral Lords. Many of the inner circle of the Nazis from Germany have now moved into this country and have infiltrated positions of control in the government and intelligence agencies. Now, YOU shall move into that area and lead these humans who are awaiting a taste of the power that will lead to world domination, and this will enable us to combat those who are not of these two dimensions and who would oppose and deter us in our purposes. It is decreed that you have passed all tests which have been given you, and now it is time for the last one. Are you now ready?"

'"Yes, I have the boy."

'"Then discard that shadow of yourself and become Razparil, so that you may leave your circle of protection."

'It was becoming obvious to my child mind that I was the last requirement of this evil pact. Fear flooded through me, and I felt no longer as a child, but as a being trapped in a child body. I tried to let go of my father's hand and suddenly I became aware that it had changed, not only in appearance, but it felt cold and wet. To my horror it was now long and bony, with long, black nails from which blood was dripping over my hand. My instant recoil had no effect of escape. I looked up, and automatically vomited. The head in the gown was the most hideous, evil mask I had ever seen. Two red eyes glowed from deep sunken sockets; the skin was yellow and drawn tightly over the facial bones, which protruded like a skeleton's. The mouth was twisted in a constant leer. I tried to pull away, but was as helpless as a puppet on a string.

'"I have brought the boy. He has not been tainted by the superficial religions and has been kept ready for this age, as agreed in my original pact."

'"Then it is time for you to give to this circle the first born of the age seven, as Belial commands you to deliver the Devil's Child. **Now! Belial awaits my return.**"

'The grotesque being could not leave its circle, and held out its claw-like hands in front of it. '

"Deliver the child!"

'Razparil began to drag me forward as I kicked back at him. I screamed out, "Noooooo!"

'My mind was alive to the danger and I commanded everything in my being to come forth and help me. But nothing came, only dark, murky spirals of dense energy. '"Noooooooo!"

'Just then the door burst open and my mother came rushing forward into the circle and grabbed my free arm. Razparil's contorted mouth screeched out, "Begone, you wretched individual!" and he twisted his body to lunge out at her.

'"The child, the child. BRING THE CHILD!"

'"You cannot do this!" screamed my mother. And Razparil's free clawed hand gouged the side of her face. Her blood gushed over my naked body and I felt the first pangs of love from the warmth of her vital fluids. Razparil was beginning to have trouble as he was now confronted on two sides, whilst Astaroth kept screaming out in the background. He let go of my hand and grabbed my mother and bodily threw her toward Astaroth. Something like an electric charge sprung from his hands, and Astaroth sent her body flying into the wall, as the smell of burning flesh filled the air.

'I ran toward the open door: I must escape, I thought. What have I done to deserve this? 'Razparil opened out his arms and, like a giant bat, flew through the air and grabbed me up.

'"Aieeee!" I screamed, and was propelled into the circle of Astaroth. Then there was darkness, for I remember nothing of what happened with Astaroth.

'The next morning I awoke in my bed. I still felt whole. Was it a dream? Even though the sun shone through the window there was no warmth in it as the air was too cold. I felt heavy and lifeless. I just wanted to cry, but no tears came. I got out of bed and looked in the mirror, and recoiled. My body was covered with dried blood, and on my left breast was a mark that burned – it was the mark of the devil.

'I never saw my mother again. Razparil had me taken straight to boarding school, and I have never seen him since either. I assume that he works in the darkness where he now manipulates the minds and emotions of those humans seeking power at a price.

'I have never forgotten what occurred that night, every word and every act, and I have constantly been taken over by grotesque beings when they want to manifest some black deed here on this dimension. I am a creature who knows not love; I have never had any friends, now or at school, college or university. I am unable to express any emotion except the destructive or negative. I don't know why I told you both this. Somehow I felt that the capsule and its message could give me some hope, or salvation, though I do not think so.'

We sat in silence, staring at Carl. I had an urge to ask certain questions but an inward voice ordered me to be silent. Instead I looked at Rose. The tears were streaming down her cheeks. I do not know whether they were tears of pity or tears of despair. I only know that I personally felt a great grief.

Rose got up. She attempted to offer Carl an arm of consolation, but almost angrily he shrugged her off.

'I think we ought to go home,' I suggested. 'Carl, you look so ill, would you like me to come with you?'

Carl shook his head. 'No— I'm okay. I'll be all right alone.'

Rose was not convinced. 'You shouldn't drive, the way you are. Let me drive you home,' she offered.

'No, goddamn it!' Carl nearly shouted. 'I'm going home now, and I'm going alone. Let me be! Let me be!'

We stood back as he lurched towards the door. We were incapable of helping him, at least today. I noticed that he had left his camera on the floor so I picked it up and put it safely in his desk drawer.

Rose had said nothing else, but had dried her eyes and was getting her own things together. I didn't want her to leave too, not yet. 'Rose,' I began, but she turned away.

'I can't handle this just now. I'll see you tomorrow. I'm sorry, Jon, but I have to deal with this by myself.'

I sighed as I watched Rose drive away. To see her so upset for Carl – the compassion for that sad, suffering being – made me like her all the more, and I wished that we could have shared a few moments of quiet together. For the first time in a long while I began to long for communion with another – and that other being Rose. We had been companionable before, so easy and relaxed, but now she seemed to be turning away.

A moment's unkindness caused me to blame Carl for this, then even the capsule and Zadore took a temporary licking, until my own better nature prevailed. I told myself I was just too darned tired and all this had really gotten to me, and I had better go home, too.

Then I realized that I had to re-record the transmission. Damn. Reluctantly, I fetched my spare cassette and prepared to do so, when I discovered that the tape had run all the way through. I had not bothered to switch the machine over, so that everything or nearly everything that Carl had said may have been recorded. I wound the tape back a way and listened to the end. By some chance Carl's very last words were there.

Should I copy this also? An inner voice said, 'Yes'. I made myself some coffee while the machine recorded, and spiked the coffee with a shot of Jack Daniels. Then, relieved this day was over – even though it was hardly yet begun – I went home.

Driving back to town, I tried not to dwell too much on what had occurred. Carl's story had eclipsed the message of the capsule somewhat, diverting my thoughts in another direction. One thing really bothered me – Carl's motives for wanting the tapes. Originally I thought he was looking toward the money he might get. Now I could not help but remember that his father and this country's intelligence agencies were connected.

CHAPTER 6

Direct Contact

For the rest of the day I did nothing but fool around aimlessly and worry about what Carl might be up to. I spent a lousy night too, which was only helped a little by the company of my old buddy, Jack Daniels.

When I arrived at the site next morning I was surprised to see Rose there. From the dark circles under her eyes I guessed she hadn't slept much either.

'I just don't know what to say or think, I just don't know,' she said sadly. 'Poor Carl. Do you think what he said was true? He would have had psychiatric counseling, wouldn't he? Maybe he just pushed it all under for all these years, and the capsule and its message brought it all back again. Jon, what are you going to do with this capsule?'

'I don't really know, Rose. Perhaps we will have the answer by the time its transmission is completed. Also I don't know whether it will activate again after it closes down. I feel that the tapes may be the only things we will end up with— and a capsule that says and does nothing.'

'How is it that only you can get the thing going?'

'It just seems to happen. It's a mystery to me as well.'

A car roared to a stop outside and a car door slammed rather too loudly. Rose and I shared an apprehensive glance. Then, trailing dust, Carl marched into the office. His face was set and hard – emotionless.

'Carl,' said Rose, 'I—'

Carl interrupted her. 'If it's about yesterday, forget it. I was not myself, and made it up. I have been on medication and also had some beer, as the weather was hot. The two seemed to interact and I cannot remember what nonsense came out. What with that and this damned capsule, it must have given me hallucinations. Anyway, what are you going to do with this thing, Jon? I don't think that you should continue recording its junk. It's probably just a hoax from the old Soviet regime.'

Carl's outburst took us both by surprise. However his last words tripped the memory of the dream experience I'd had a couple of nights before. This aroused my suspicions about Carl. I had better heed the warning of Zadore.

'Rose and I were just discussing the capsule. Personally, I think we should continue with the recording until we hear the full message, and only then can we really decide whether it's a hoax or not.'

'I agree with Jon,' said Rose.

I was glad of Rose's support, especially if Carl was going to be difficult.

'Well, Carl?'

As if he did not care one way or another, Carl shrugged. 'It looks like I'm out voted. I'll sit in and listen. But I'm sure that you will see that I'm right and it's a hoax.'

It was pointless to argue such a foolish theory, so I let it go. No one asked any more why I was the only one who could activate the capsule. Perhaps they believed I was a Communist. I thought that was a laugh. I set the tape recorder going and we all sat in front of the capsule. Presently it began to glow and I had a sudden, silent thought: We know that this is a transmitter. I wonder if it is a receiver as well. That would be interesting.

THE EARTH SPEAKS:

'**Y**ou have listened to much that has been said about my birth and growth – you have now spread across my surface in your billions. What you do not realize is that I allowed your entrance into my matter for you to assist me in my growth and the deepening of my conscious contact with the Galaxy, the same place where you come from. Now you have forgotten your purpose and seek to dominate my expression of light. In your greed you have weakened the ozone layer that was developed to protect all life forms including that which you occupy. As the intensity of the rays of my Mother Sun now penetrate more deeply into my interior, it will drive your race to move your dwelling places under the ground. Such a move will alter your morphogenetic patterns and weaken them to such an extent that the majority of your bodies will be terminated.

What you must understand from this is that I am your salvation, and that only through me will you be able to develop your Light or Soul Body! Once you do this you will be free to work as Gods in the Universe. Your time is running out— you must decide now!(7)

It is time to surrender the sensual needs of your Ego and become loving to me and make amends for that which you have destroyed. The Lords of Karma demand this.

Once you have forgiven yourself and turn to the light of your own being, love and light will flow once more through my human bodies, healing them of the sickness imposed on them for many millennia. They will be perfect again, as they were when I created them.'

ZADORE SPEAKS:

'The Earth is powered by the light and consciousness that originates in the center of the Galaxy and flows through the Sun. As you have already heard, the two radiation belts moved away from the Earth's surface as the planet began to cool. Once the waters were in place, the solar winds buffeted the planet, producing a magnetic field, and the cone-shaped cavity thus formed is called the magnetosphere. The solar wind is an outflow of ionized particles, which carry the information to the Earth not only from the Sun but from all other star systems in the Galaxy.

This information includes that energy which has often been referred to as the Life Force, however it is actually Light Force.

Over millions of years there have been many changes to the Earth's climate which have been responsible for the evolving consciousness or maturing of the Earth as a living organism. There have been periods of ice ages, floods, volcanic and earthquake changes, all of which were initiated by the Sun. Each change caused a cleansing of the various life forms, either by extinction, or by adaptation to the altered climate and environment. This resulted in more complex forms able to transmit higher information. What must be made common knowledge is that those forces which control all the various governments of the planet are creating many of the climate changes that are overriding the natural progression. They are creating earthquakes and other warming conditions, which are destined to destroy habitable life.

There are other cyclic changes initiated by the Sun, the smallest one being a cycle of approximately 11.3 Earth years. These short term changes are monitored by peaks of activity which occur when great flares of incandescent gas move away from the Sun's surface. This acts as an on/off switch to the Earth, creating energy changes to the Earth.

The last reversal occurred in 1990, and the next change will be in 2001. Such polarity shifts cause aberrant patterns in the frequency bands around the Earth, and these patterns create frequency shifts to the Earth's magnetic fields.

Such cycles as these are minute in comparison to the greater cycles of the Galaxy. This solar system involves a 25 million year orbit around the center of the Milky Way. Time in a universal sense does not exist, all Being is in Light.

More will follow.'

The capsule ceased transmission and stopped glowing.

'There you go,' remarked Carl. 'What a short transmission that was. I still think that this should be handed over to the authorities, who will soon tear it apart to reveal it as the hoax it is.'

'Who would you give it to?' enquired Rose. 'The C.I.A., of course. They would know best.'

This was not a subject I wanted to get drawn into.

'I think it's time we went out to the trench to make up some of the hours we've spent on this project.

We can discuss everything later,' I said.

We spent the whole day measuring and marking out a new trench, only returning to the office for lunch, and to quit. I would have locked the capsule away in case anyone was tempted, but no one mentioned it. I believe we were all a tiny bit conscience stricken about having neglected our duties.

Although I worked hard that day I still found it difficult to concentrate. Carl was constantly on my mind. Which story of his was true? Was any of it believable? Yet Carl was certainly a strange character and such a story as his was surely too fantastic to have been invented, even by a hallucinating brain. I knew I could not trust Carl but was at a loss to decide what he might be planning. Finally, at 4.00P.M., seeing how tired Rose appeared, I suggested we call it a day. No one argued.

When the other two had safely driven off to town, I hurried to make my transmission copy. Then I decided not to go home right away. I had some extra paperwork to finalize – the burden of being a team leader – and besides, what or who was there in my life to go home to?

It must have been about 6.00P.M. when I finished. I sat back in my chair to consider just how lives and relationships can be changed in a short time by events. I began to reflect on the communication from Zadore, and the Sun and Earth. I wondered at the conceptual changes the message brought and how such changes would influence our understanding of the Earth and, for that matter, the Universe itself.

So deep in thought was I that I did not notice the capsule glowing. I first became aware of it as a blue haze in front of my eyes. It became quite bright with dusk descending outside. I turned toward the capsule, surprised to see the hologram of Zadore appearing. What the hell is happening? I thought. I didn't concentrate to activate it!

Astonishingly, Zadore addressed me directly; as if he knew I was alone:

'Jon Whistler, it is time for you to begin to understand what you are required to do. But firstly you must see to the recording machine, as I do not want this message to be forgotten by you.'

Zadore waited – a patient flame dancing in the dusk, while I did as he asked. To me, this was amazing because it made me suspect that somehow he was with me in the room, as an ordinary person might be. There was more to this capsule business than I had otherwise believed.

'Yes, Jon, you think truly,' said Zadore, answering my unspoken thought. 'Now you have to understand this – you have been denying yourself for many years. Immersed in the worldly illusion of your senses, you have forgotten your true spirit. You were surprised to learn that this communication capsule is a two-way unit, however, earlier, your intuition suggested this but you dismissed it. That is what is wrong, you listen too much to reason and not to yourself.'

'You are communicating with me directly through the capsule? You're not just a computer hologram?' I asked, incredulous.

'What you see before you is a hologram and the capsule is a computer, but not in the sense of computers developed on Earth, which are very basic. Through it I can transmit information and receive it. Should the capsule fall into the hands of your public authorities, and if they could open it at all, then they would discover nothing in it but light, not just ordinary light, but light of such a frequency that it would destroy their physical bodies. When the last transmission is received by you, you must return the capsule to the place where you found it, and within twenty four hours it will melt back into the ethers.'

'Melt?'

I was confused and a little dismayed by this last statement. 'You mean the capsule will be destroyed? You must know that Carl, Rose and I have been discussing its future, but now you say that there is nothing to be done but to return it to the countryside here. Then what is the purpose of your transmission, and why did it come to us in this way?'

'Jon, you have the answer already, but you do not see it. You are still placing your trust in outer things and you feel that you need the capsule to give credence to the tapes. But the capsule is not important. Nor are the tape recordings important except that they are an aid to you in remembering what you have been told.
Jon, you must learn from the tapes. You must take them to your home and listen to the message they offer. That is what is truly important, Jon Whistler, that you learn from the tapes – and what you learn will be that YOU are the message.'

'I?'

'**Y**es, Jon. The nature of the message is such that individuals on this planet, who are ready to receive what it conveys, will need no proof apart from the words. They will allow it to activate their consciousness and strike in them a chord of understanding, which will propel them forward into that realm of consciousness that will save the planet from destruction.

'You will soon come to an understanding of what your future work involves, and see that it is the taking of this communication to the world. But first you must take the communication into yourself. You cannot communicate the change until you become the change. The message will create a quickening in your neural patterns, opening your consciousness into the realities of the Universe.

Without this adjustment within you, the message will have no meaning and will be just another oracle that provides intellectual gratification, followed by platitudes. This is a living message that will live in and activate the hearts and minds of those who embrace it.

'Presently you are confused and show concern about what your two friends are thinking and doing relative to the communication. Their fears and behavior reflect your own inner turmoil, and you are not outwardly aware of it. Meditate on this, and begin to understand that what you see in others holds up a mirror to yourself. The good you see in others only reflects the good in yourself, so too does the bad. This is your first understanding in your integration with your Light Body. For until you surrender your Ego, and allow your true essence to be revealed, and give it power, you cannot begin the change, for the change awaits you.

Once you turn your back on all the illusions that your Ego amplifies, both your mind and body will shine with your Light, eliminating all the sickness attached to mind and body. Then, and only then, will you see what you are, and what you will then see,

Jon, is that you are ME – Zadore – and all those who return to the Light of themselves are also ME. It is timely that you now begin to listen to the tapes regularly in order that you understand the message. This message will help to move out of your present frequency of consciousness, that level of frequency which binds you and all others and keeps you trapped in the time loop set up by the Astral Entities.'

All of this was blowing my brain.

'But Zadore how is it possible for me to change so quickly? I've never gone in for metaphysics or the like – I've no special training, and I don't particularly care for spiritual exercises or disciplines.'

Zadore listened patiently to my objections and excuses then replied:

'Jon that is your illusion. In fact, that is also the illusion held by many of those who practise such exercises and disciplines. In the mistaken understanding that these will free them spiritually, they bind themselves to this or that doctrine, and their rituals become limitations. Many live in the belief that they can perfect themselves this way and many also believe that they must continually return to another body to complete their regeneration. How foolish they are to think that a mastery of the Third-dimension frequency sets them free without any further obligation. Every dimension has its challenges to precipitate growth. What you must realize is that already you are a majestic being of Light, only you deny it. It is your Ego that maintains this denial, for it does not want anything else to be seen as being greater than it is.

'For, all who are trapped in the physical bodies, and sleep in the Fourth-dimension, they cannot see or define that which is Ego. Your Ego is not a thing or entity. It may be likened to a lens that allows your Light to pass through in a concentrated manner. It

59

is a grounding device, which reflects the Earth's bodies and atmosphere to your consciousness. However, Mankind has been taught that what is seen through this lens is the true state and that the world of matter is the individual playground for the Ego. Through the five bodily senses all this is reflected through to the mind in the body, and this then creates the Illusion. It becomes a constant battle for the Ego-centered body to dim the Light that you really are. Because you accept that you are this body, your Ego pretends that the actions of others affect you. You consider that you are greater than others, that you can be hurt, or your pride can be hurt. Your Ego tells you that you should fear extinction and death, and, in fact, when you do something that you know is wrong, your Ego chastises you and makes you suffer, lowering your self expression and self esteem. All this, to turn you away from seeing the control and illusion of the Third- dimension.

'What you need to do is accept yourself, and have your Ego surrender to the unconditional love that you should express daily. Learn to love others and judge them not, for you are only judging yourself.'

'You are saying that I am not what I think I am?' I questioned.

'You are not your illusion, Jon. You are the I AM – that is all – and until you seek wisdom and Light from the I AM, you dwell in a darkness of your own making. You must learn to feel with your heart and mind. Do not think with your intellect, but just feel and BE IT.'

It seemed that Zadore was about to end this dialogue between us, so I asked, 'How much longer will the transmissions go on? I think Carl and Rose are becoming impatient, and Carl, I'm sure, has other ideas for the capsule and tapes.'

'Transmission will cease when its ending occurs. Time has no value in the realm of Light. Carl and Rose will wait until the final message is completed, and it is necessary that you be aware of their intentions. Rose is not negative toward the communication. She is confused at present, like you; it is a matter of Ego. However, she will warm to the teaching and convey much of what she feels to you.

'Carl, an unfortunate being, has been unjustly used by the creatures of darkness for their nefarious needs. Since a child, he has been inwardly instructed in their ways, and they led him to your company in order to prevent these transmissions from being exposed to the masses. This is the end-point of their possession – that he be their agent at this time – nothing else.

'Do not condemn him, for his karma is heavy, and this life has been a result of past mistakes. The transmission has marked a change to his inner struggle, and he will, in a future time, grow in his own Light. His story is true, and it was revealed to you two in order that you understand that Razparil will work at the destruction of your attempt to generate this message. However, do not fear this Astral devil, for his power is lessening daily.

'When the time is right I will project through all dimensions a Vortex of Light and Healing which will draw to it all those seeking to move towards their Light and God-head. There will be further transmissions.

'I will leave you now.'

CHAPTER 7

The Time Wave

I can best describe how profoundly this last transmission from Zadore affected me by saying that I drove home in a dream and cannot remember if I stopped at any red lights, as I was supposed to do. I guess I must have, automatically, since I never received a ticket afterward, but the entire journey is lost to me.

My consciousness was definitely out of this world that night, although everything I contemplated as I drove blindly home was more than pertinent to the world I knew – it was absolutely vital. Many questions ran through my head, and many doubts too. Such as, 'Was I really the right person for this job?' I was not a writer in the popular sense. Beyond my reports and a few technical papers, which were in formal, scientific language, I had never attempted any creative writing, and I realized even then that the transmissions would need an acceptable setting – something to explain their telling. And what about publicity and promotion? It was not within my scope and I was not sure I wanted it to be. Also, I still clung to the erroneous belief that the capsule itself was the best promotion for the tapes. But Zadore had scotched that option. At that point of time I did not understand what Zadore meant by the message being ME. I had not felt the change as yet. I did not know what a potent thing it would be. I also could not foresee the events that would take me through the change, which would *force* me through, in fact.

I wondered greatly at what Zadore had said about Carl. By stating that Carl had been led purposely into my company, Zadore was telling me that this role I was supposed to take on had been foretold. It had to have been; I had known Carl for many years before this. That fact amazed me then, but later on I was able to see from a different perspective. Then, I was still a creature of neat little boxes; time, place, past, future, present, you, me, it – everything separate and tidy – I had not begun yet to flow with the Universe.

At home I continued to dream. I showered, changed, cooked, ate – all unconsciously, or consciously somewhere else. I even stared for a while at the T.V. while it paraded its usual disasters, but the only effect it had on me was to drive me into contemplation of our world. Certainly we needed to change the way of the world. In the U.S., while many of us lived a reasonable and even lavish lifestyle, there were a whole lot of us who did not; and as for personal safety – well, life was okay, as long as we could protect ourselves from each other.

And what about the world at large? Where could you go now and be safe to walk alone at night, or, in some areas, even in the day? There was no doubt in my mind that society was close to hitting rock bottom, and that some kind of change was necessary.

But the change could not be a materialistic one – like a revolution or an uprising. Besides, such events never alter the world; they merely exchange one misery for another, one set of oppressors for another. No, the change must be in Human Consciousness and, as Zadore told me, it must be a healing change and an absolute freeing from all the illusions of the past and present. It would be a major shift in the consciousness of Being on this planet.

This change was going to be major! And this change was

relying on me to start it happening!

ME! 'Why me?' I asked. 'I'm just an ordinary guy, and I didn't ask for this to happen.'

'No,' said an inner voice. 'You are not ordinary. No one is ordinary – you are all Beings of Light. And I did ask. I have been asking for centuries, only you have taken no notice of my voice because you were focused on the Illusion and thought yourself separate from me.'

'But I still feel separate,' I argued with my inner voice. 'And alone, too. I feel this is going to be a burden to me and I'm not sure how well I'll shoulder it. I wish I had some help.'

'You do,' the voice replied. 'You are not alone. Don't forget – others are at this moment experiencing thoughts and feelings about the message of the capsule. You are not alone.'

'Well, I can't count on Carl,' I told myself. 'He is so twisted up by his past that he doesn't know what he's doing. But Rose may help – Zadore said she could. I wish Rose was here now. I'd like to share this with her.'

I considered giving Rose a call, but when I looked at my watch I saw that it was already 11.30P.M.. Where had the hours gone? And, oh boy, I was tired all of a sudden. I went to bed, thinking of Rose. I sure would have loved to get together with her and talk this thing out properly. I remembered how, when I first met Rose, I had fancied us getting together in another way, but had been too much of a backward idiot to do anything about it. So I had settled for friendship and, I felt, that was what Rose herself had chosen. After all, she was a bit of a youngster compared with me, and would obviously prefer guys more her own age.

My head filled with nonsense, I finally went to sleep. However I slept badly and it was dreams of earthquakes and holes in the ground that troubled me most of the night. I realized in the morning that this was because I was feeling guilty about wasted work hours, so I decided that from now on it would be best to leave the capsule in the cabinet until after our workday was over.

I had no objections from the others over my decision and we went to the trenches without argument. Without any conversation as far as Carl was concerned, for he seemed disinclined to communicate at all with either Rose or me. However, when we returned to the office that evening he was much more relaxed. At least he appeared so and, surprisingly, was quite eager to hear the next transmission.

ZADORE SPEAKS:

'You have now learnt much about the birth of the planet and the influence of the Sun in its continued growth. You have also been informed about the radiation belts and their containment of the morphogenetic fields where the various patterns for life and growth are stored for use in the development of all matter or form on the planet, including the patterns that your bodies are currently matched with. Other things have been touched on briefly, such as the Astral Lords, and the conscious seeding of the Earth bodies from the star systems throughout the Galaxy. I now want to create in your consciousness a broader or enlarged picture of what has led us to the current time frame on this planet. Once you understand this you will know what you need to do to rectify the destructive pattern that Humanity is running head first into.

The Galaxy is a spiraling mass of stars in the Universe, in which the Earth is a small speck. The Sun is the center of the star system that you call the Solar System. Throughout the Galaxy there are thousands of other star systems. All these star systems have a central sun, and all these suns focus the Light of the Universe through themselves. They act as lenses, in that they beam the Light Consciousness of Light directionally to the planets in their specific system, as well as to other stars.

In other words, with your third-dimensional vision the Sun appears to you as being a ball of light. To the scientist, it is filled with incandescent gases. The Creative Light of all the Universes flows directly through these suns, and all the suns are virtual star gates to another universe, different from the one which your consciousness currently experiences. These star gates are the doorways to the Fifth-dimension.

The dimensional universe that you daily perceive is the Third-dimensional universe, which is counter-balanced by the Fourth-dimension. In actuality, the Third and Fourth dimensions form one universe. The difference between them is a matter of polarity. This Universe, which comprises many galaxies and solar systems, contains both Third and Fourth dimensional consciousness. That is, these dimensions throughout the Universe are composed of energies of a specific density, the Third-dimension being more dense than the Fourth. The energy frequencies that flow through the Sun are Fifth-dimensional frequencies and higher. These energy frequencies flow constantly from Light Itself.

There is no separation of dimension, as all dimensions mold into one another. However, at specific frequency levels higher rates of consciousness exist. When living in a Third-dimensional frequency such as on this planet, you view the dimension through your five senses, which are attached to the frequency of the body, utilizing an Ego to relate the impressions from the senses, through the brain and glands to your higher dimensional frequencies, for interpretation. Depending on just how the Ego presents this information is how all the problems on this planet develop.

The Third-dimension is not limited to the density of the physical body alone. There are a series of levels of energy that move up to the level of the Ego. These higher levels of energy have been termed Etheric. They should be termed Life Energies, or even Life Body Energies. As you move your consciousness beyond the level of these life energies, you move into the Fourth-dimension, of which the Astrals occupy some of its levels. The various levels increase in frequency until you move into the Fifth-dimension. The Fourth-dimension can be loosely termed as being the Feeling Frequency. The Fifth-dimension is a light frequency; the lowest level is represented by the suns of the Universe.

Before the seeding, which is known as the convergence of light consciousness from the many star systems in the Galaxy, there was an entry of another consciousness into Earth's frequency. This was not a voluntary entrance into these two dimensions, for the beings of this other consciousness were imprisoned here by the Galactic Lords, as they had attempted to gain control, by force, of the Galactic Gate, which is the center of this Galaxy and the source of all light for this Galaxy from Light. They were expelled to the Fourth-dimension of this Solar System to choose their future, and their choice has been obvious relative to their actions in the Solar System. When you access the memory banks in the radiation belts of this planet, you will find that to the Earth consciousness these beings have been defined in the Luciferian myths. They were cast out from their high position close to the central core of the Galaxy, to the Fourth-dimension of this Solar System. They were moved through the Sun and radiation belts and clothed in bodies much like Earth bodies, but of a less dense nature.

Being Fourth-dimensional beings, they could not experience the separation that occurs on the Third-dimension. They observed the processes of life formation on the Third-dimension, and how the morphogenetic patterns were transferred from the Sun to the outer radiation belts and reflected to the Earth, relative to the expansion of the Earth's consciousness.

They watched the Elemental Beings pass through the Sun to the Earth, attaching themselves to the morphogenetic patterns as they descended to the Earth. They were amazed that, even though they could see these beings, they could not communicate with them, and this angered them immensely. These Elemental Beings work selflessly to maintain, against all odds, the continual patterning of the forms. They also set in place the various rock formations, plants, trees, water, clouds, thunderstorms, insects, fish, and animals, including human form.

Some of the older religions revered these Elementals, and in many instances they were worshiped. The older races of the

Earth, and even some of the current civilization, would ask permission of these spirits to hunt and kill animals, or each other; to cut down trees and to take all other needs from Nature. Other religions referred to the Elementals as fairies or angels. One particular religion called the Elementals, who are responsible for the maintenance of the form of the human body, guardian angels. This myriad of light beings are constantly working through the Third and Fourth dimensional universes to maintain the patterns of Light. They are quite distinct from other light beings such as yourselves.

When some of the primitive patterns of animal organisms were formed by the Earth, the Astrals experimented by projecting their consciousness to these forms. In a small sense of the word, they began what could be called the first seeding of the planet. It had an accelerating effect on the frequencies of the organisms, however, due to the negative nature of the Astrals, this seeding imparted unwanted frequencies into the DNA light strands of the organisms, and still these manifest in all physical bodies of both animal and human. Mankind often refers to these negative frequencies as instincts. Such frequencies alter the personality and lead to aggressive behavior patterns, which were not originally found in the morphogenetic fields. In particular, the emotion of fear is a good example of such a negative frequency.

Such a grounding excited the Astrals. For the first time they felt a sense of separation from their light form and began to express their emotional feelings on a definite plane – it was like being reborn. This duality allowed them to manipulate some of the prime patterns of the planet. They believed that if they could take control of the patterns, thereby taking control of the outer consciousness that would be projected to these forms, then they would gain power to move once more deeper into the Galaxy. Although they could move their consciousness into the Earth bodies, they could not alter the form to suit their needs, for these forms originated beyond the Fourth-dimension, to which their power was limited. Another problem they experienced with their experiment was that all these body forms had a limited period before they broke down and their essence returned to formative matter. They saw this as a limiting potential of the Third-dimensional frequency. Everything in Light moves continually through cycles of emergence and return, from and to the source. The Third-dimensional Universe follows this cycle, but at differing time spans, depending on the entity. The Astrals could not perfect their move to the Third-dimension, for they had to continually move their consciousness into new forms at an increasing rate, without forgetting their purpose.

They found from their Inter-dimensional experience that they could duplicate many of the Earth's morphogenetic patterns on the Fourth-dimension. However, they could not maintain the structure of the forms, as the Elemental Beings would not have any contact with them.

As well, they could not maintain the projection of their consciousness to the Third-dimension, as it was depleting their energies. So they ended their experiment. Now they had produced some major problems for the Earth, for they had planted a virtual disease in the patterns that, unknown at the time to the Astrals, would work in their favor when future seeding took place. Their negative frequencies remained in the Earth's patterns and, due to the constant reproduction of the patterns, had become part and parcel of the reproduction process. No amount of attempts by the Earth to rid these taints could be achieved, even after floods, earthquakes or ice ages. The current wave of consciousness that moves through the human bodies has to deal with these taints, and it has been one of the major reasons for your forgetting of your purpose and turning to the Illusion that the Astrals presented you with.

THE ILLUSION:

'Prior to your current civilization there have been other periods where the Race attained equal and, in some areas, greater levels of achievement in technology. From these previous out-flows from the Fifth-dimension there are still some of those beings projecting or incarnating in Earth bodies. When the Astrals found that their projection into matter was not a fruitful exercise, they waited for the time when the current wave of consciousness began to move through their dimension to the Earth. For many thousands of years the Astrals watched the progression of those consciousnesses, as they began to express themselves on the lower dimension. At that time the Ego acted as a lens, which transmitted their experiences back from the Earth, and vice versa. At this juncture the Ego acted as a consciousness for the body's survival and awareness of its environment.

Being aware of the potential taint that they previously infused into the old patterns, the Astrals were able to communicate with these beings on that level and only through dream states. However, the bodies spent all the hours of darkness in the dream realm, and the Astrals were able to constantly promote feelings of fear and separation, which would eventually spill over into the waking consciousness.

This created in the Ego consciousness a feeling of the need for survival in such a dense environment, and, by drawing the consciousness of the Ego into a greater dependence upon their advice, the Astrals became to that consciousness as Gods or Oracles, and were more and more consulted, through dreams and trance states, for help in coping with a hostile-seeming world.

This pattern of dependence was repeated and perfected by the Astrals over many aeons of time, becoming more precise and efficient in the repetition. As I have just said, some of Earth's previous civilizations reached a peak of technological achievement such that they disrupted the Earth's balance in their attempts to control nature, and thus they caused the destruction of their own civilizations.

Then, lost in misery and fear and ignorance and savagery, they returned to the rebuilding stage again, and to the dependence upon Astral advice. These constant backward steps were ideal for the Astrals, as the continual replaying of the pattern only strengthened it and, consequently, Astral influence and control.

The Illusion of the Astrals was in the convincing of the Egos that they (the Egos), were the most powerful beings in the Universe, and that their mission was to understand and control the Earth and use the Earth for their power and potential to become as Gods. The Illusion was designed to show the Ego consciousness that all power was obtained through developing the senses and the intellect, to build and destroy, to wield the power of life and death.

The second Illusion was an after-death Illusion, and it was created on the lower levels of the Fourth-dimension. Much of what has been achieved on the Earth by the Human Egos was duplicated in the Fourth-dimension. This means all worldly aspects such as houses, gardens, libraries, colleges and research laboratories, and all forms of amusement and entertainment, and ranges up to lofty ideals and everything that is desired on the Earth as expressing a Kingdom of Heaven. The Astrals have created crystal palaces and Beings of Light and Peace, and once these wonderful things have been experienced in great joy by the unsuspecting Ego, it falls asleep in the Illusion and eventually returns back to a new existence on the Earth.

This after-death Illusion allows the Astrals to contain and control the massive amount of energy that is constantly given freely by those trapped in this illusion of the senses. The whole quest of the
Astrals is to break free from their own bondage, and they care nothing about how they achieve their results.

As they viewed the Earth's crystal structure, it reminded them of the crystal rays that flow through the Galaxy. These crystal rays or strands are the communicating links which flow through the Universe. The Earth contains solid crystal structures, of which there are eight different lattices which are responsible for all the mineral elements that compose its structure. Therefore the Earth is an important link in the Galaxy, for it encodes and grounds information for further processing and transmission. The Astrals have been using some of the Earth's energies to transport elements to different parts of the planet. In fact, those Humans who became Astral entities, themselves used this power to build the old stone monuments on behalf of the Astrals. These stone structures have a high crystalline structure, which was used by the Astrals to communicate beyond the radiation belts, in seeking accord with others of like mind in the Galaxy. This resulted in an influx of extra-terrestrials on this planet.

Once again the Astrals have led the consciousness of the Earth beings to a point of power and achievement. This time they did not want to fail. Again they are prepared for war, a war that they expect will give them the power to break free from their tomb. They, through cooperation with many of the major governments of this world, are currently perfecting the nuclear bombs and know the exact grid-points whereby these will cause the most effective damage to the planet and its potential for further growth. It is fast reaching a point where they will give an ultimatum to the Galactic Lords – 'Free Us, or we destroy this Planet!' The decision for the Galactic Lords has been difficult, and they have only two choices. The first is to tilt the planet and destroy again all life here and start again. Or the second, which is to send this message to re-awaken you to send all the Neo-Astrals – those humans who have given their souls to the Astral, devils – to their imprisonment with their Astral cohorts, and cleanse the Ego of all the taints of evil.

Already the Sun is instituting those measures to protect its child, and you will see this as increasing changes of climate, as earthquakes, volcanic upheavals and drought and all other changes that will quickly reduce the Earth bodies. When the previous Earth changes were precipitated by the civilizations of the day, the Astrals retreated back to the Fourth-dimension, to await another time, and this time is at hand. The re-awakening is the preferred choice of the Galactic Lords, and this message must reach out to touch those who are now ready. That is the important work for you. That is why the capsule was centered toward you three, for you all are necessary in its completion. You will learn more about the past mistakes in the next transmission.'

Another transmission brought itself to a close. In the fading light we sat in silence. I had the sudden urge not to do as we usually did and leave matters as they were, but provoke some sort of comment. Rose seemed to glow warmly. Obviously the message was having a positive effect on her consciousness. Carl looked surly again. What was going on in that muddled head of his? I would like to know.

'There's certainly a lot to think about,' I said. 'Especially that last part. Anyone like to say something?'

'About what?' said Carl abruptly. 'You know what I think of the whole business – it's rubbish.'

Carl was beginning to get on my nerves. 'You seem interested enough…in rubbish,' I could not help saying in a sarcastic voice.

Carl glared at me angrily but did not reply. 'I'm going home,' he snapped, and got up and left. 'Well done,' said Rose wryly.

Annoyed, not by Rose but by my own ineptitude in dealing with Carl, I rose to my own defense. 'It's irritating, the way he derides what is said when you know he really believes it.'

'That's why he derides it,' said Rose. 'You can see that, can't you? He's afraid of the truths and what they mean for him. He's terrified by them, because of his past life and his father.'

Rose and I had not discussed Carl's story at all, and I had wondered if Rose believed his lie of the next day.

'I'm sure his story is true,' said Rose. 'There's too much horror in it for even the weirdest imagination. Poor Carl, you have to feel sorry for him, and take his past into consideration.'

Chastened, I nodded. 'I do feel sorry for him. I pity him terribly. But I am also wary of him, and I'd like to tell you why. I'd like to talk about other things, too – the capsule and the message – what it all means. I need to talk with you.'

Rose smiled at me then. 'I'm glad, because I need to talk to you, too. I've been trying to think how to say it for a while. There is so much welling up in me that I have to get it out, or I'll burst!'

'I didn't know you felt that way, Rose,' I replied. 'You've been so silent and self contained these last few days. I thought you didn't want to talk.'

'I thought the same way about you, Jon,' said Rose, and we both smiled at our own absurdity. 'How about a meal then?' I asked her.

'Food and talk? That's a great idea. That new Diner on the way back to town serves good food, and Thursday night ought not to be too crowded. Want to go there?'

'Sounds fine to me. Let's go.'

CHAPTER 8

Old Nations

The diner was bright, spacious and not too noisy or crowded. I had never eaten there before and was pleased by the clean, open atmosphere. The waitresses, all older women with friendly smiles, were a cheery, garrulous lot. One, a fifty-something gal named Gloria, led us to our table and on the way she chatted with Rose as if they were old friends.

Before we had even glanced at the menu, she said: 'Seafood's good tonight. Tempura or beer batter?'

'Oh, beer, definitely,' said Rose. Obviously Rose was a regular and the waitress knew her preferences in food.

Then Rose, with a wicked glint in her eye, introduced me as her boss.

Gloria gave me an odd, amused grin. 'So you dig holes for living, too, do ya?' I was somewhat nonplussed. 'Er— yes, I guess you could put it that way, I do.'

After Gloria had taken our orders to the kitchen I protested to

Rose. 'I'm not your boss, Rose!'

Rose laughed. 'I know. But it impresses them. They're a bit old-fashioned – the girls here. Didn't think it was quite kosher for a young woman to be running all over the countryside in the company of two guys, digging holes!'

'That's what you told them you do?' I laughed too, at the picture she must have painted for the bemused waitresses.

'I kind of told them that, although I did try to explain. But they just didn't get it. Don't think they believed me either. But now they will…or they'll have something to gossip about at least.'

'Why should they believe me any better?' I asked, still laughing.

Rose looked at me strangely. The light in her eyes, this time I could not understand. 'Well, I think they will. I think you are a pretty believable sort of guy.' She paused to smile at me. 'And you know, it's kind of nice to see you laughing for a change. I've been a bit worried about you lately.'

Suddenly I felt a warm glow inside. 'Since I found the capsule, you mean?' 'Yes.'

'Well, it's been a disturbing thing for all of us, I think,' I replied.

'That's true.' Rose's smile vanished and a slight frown replaced it. 'But for you I sense something more involved, and it makes me concerned. Even Carl's reaction, shocking as it is, is less profound than yours seems to be to me. Am I reading you right, Jon, or am I mistaken?'

I don't remember if I blushed then, although I think I might have. It was not her candid observation that threw me – I like honesty in a person – but the fact that she had observed me closely and so well. Also the fact that I was pleased by the knowledge and warmed by it. If another person, say Carl for instance, had said this, I might not have been so happy.

'You're reading me right,' I confessed. 'A lot has been going on and it's what I wanted to talk to you about. But you had things you wanted to say, too.'

'Oh, they can wait. Except, let's get Carl out of the way first. Why is he bothering you so much?' 'Okay. I want to talk about

Carl; however there is something else I have to tell you before. It's important that you should know.' Curiosity flooded her face. 'What?'

I described my last evening's experience with Zadore. Rose's eyes had opened wide as she listened.

'So the capsule is a receiver too! I'd never have thought it possible. It must have given you quite a shock, Zadore just popping up like that.'

'It sure did. And to realize he knew I was alone…that he was speaking to me directly, as you are now.'

Rose looked thoughtful. 'That must be the case every time then, and the capsule is not a recorder, as Carl thinks it is, but is just a medium of communication between Zadore and us. Do you think Zadore would speak to me if I asked him a question?'

I had not thought of that possibility. However I did not feel that our regular transmissions were meant to be interrupted by questioning and I also sensed that Zadore would not want Carl to know this. I said as much to Rose and she appeared a trifle disappointed.

'That's a shame. I have a lot of questions I'd love to ask. But you say that you don't want Carl knowing. He worries you a lot. Why?'

I had not mentioned what Zadore had said about Carl, nor, for that matter, Rose herself. I told her then that Zadore had confirmed Carl's horror story as true, and informed her that Carl had been purposely planted in my way so that Razparil could prevent the transmissions ever reaching Humanity. At my words, Rose seemed to falter and her face paled. 'Oh, Jon, you mean that ghastly thing is involved in all this too?'

'I'm afraid so,' I said. 'If Razparil is one of those Astral Entities Zadore speaks of, then you know he has a lot to lose if the transmissions become public.'

Nervously, Rose bit her lip. 'Yes. But Carl's story…Razparil is such a…monster…I hadn't thought…' Her words trailed away and she began fiddling with her cutlery.

I did not like to think of Rose being afraid and I guessed that she was. 'Does the idea frightened you, Rose? Zadore said we must not fear Razparil – that his power is decreasing with every day.'

Rose shuddered. 'I hope so. I won't be afraid if you're not. Are you?'

'No, I don't feel afraid,' I reassured her. I was telling the truth; I had no cause to fear Razparil – not then.

To change the subject slightly and get us away from thoughts of fear, I spoke about Carl. 'I don't trust him. From what Zadore says, Carl is likely to try to steal the capsule and the tapes for the intelligence agency his father was connected with. However there's something else he doesn't know about the capsule.'

'What's that?'

I reminded her of Zadore's earliest instructions regarding the disposal of the capsule and told her how it would simply melt and vanish into nothingness within twenty-four hours of the last transmission. Rose looked astonished but she caught on right away.

'Carl will make a fuss when he finds that out,' she said. 'Like I said before, he thinks it is a recorder. He told me that he is convinced that all he has to do is work out how to open it to get at the mechanism and the information stored inside. He will want to have a go at the before it disappears for good.'

'Zadore warned about the danger of trying that,' I informed her. 'He said it would destroy anyone who opened it, that is if they could manage it at all, which I doubt.'

'That's a relief,' sighed Rose. 'I know Carl is a problem – in the past I always thought he was a bit strange and could never really feel a great liking for him – but now I know what a rough time he's had of life, it's hard to think too unkindly of him, or judge him either.'

How gentle Rose is, I thought. What a heart. I was about to say something in reply, which, in retrospect, I realize that coming from me then would most probably have embarrassed her, when the waitress arrived with our meal. The moment was broken while Gloria stopped to chat of trivialities, then we were left alone again. There was a silence for a time until we had satisfied the first pangs of hunger and then our conversation began again in earnest.

I wanted to know what Rose thought about the transmissions, but she refused to say anything until she had found out my feelings. In the discussion of Carl I had temporarily forgotten how concerned she was over my state of mind and I did not to realize then how determined she was to seek it out.

I told her of my first, almost subconscious stirring of memory and emotion, of the sudden flood of awakening that seemed to overtake my reason and senses. I spoke of the wonder I felt when listening to the Sun and Earth – how beautiful and astonishing were the concepts I had heard, but that all this was marred somewhat by the contradictions of a scientific education and my own feelings of separation, which would not go away. 'It's hard, Rose, to break the thinking of a lifetime. I've been trained to think in certain ways about the world and about myself, and now I'm asked to blow all that away. Something in me wants to and it's like there's a vision there just ahead, but I can't quite grasp it. I sense that being able to grasp it depends on my letting go of something else, and I don't know what that something is yet.'

Rose nodded slowly. It seemed to me that her expression for me was a compassionate one, as if she thought that, not unlike Carl I needed some kindly consideration. 'Do you feel that this vision would give you freedom?' she asked softly.

Without thought or hesitation, I said, 'Yes!' I was very surprised by this because I realized immediately that she had hit the nail on the head. 'You understand,' I said appreciatively. 'You're wiser than I am then.'

'No, Jon.' Rose smiled. 'I have a different upbringing to you, that's all. Remember, I am part Hopi, and my spiritual upbringing was wholly that. The Hopi have a much closer relationship with the Earth and Creation than Europeans generally do. To the Hopi, the Earth is the Mother and through the Mother we reach out to all of life. And Life is Everything. To us, everything lives – the Rain, the Sun, our Earth Mother, the Thunder, even the Dust Storms and the Rainbow. There is no division between Spirit and Matter, and so nothing is separate. For ourselves it is the

79

same – we are not separate from one another nor from the rest of Being.'

I had to ask: 'Do you truly feel that, Rose? It's not just a religious concept?'

'I truly feel it,' said Rose, with another smile. 'Although sometimes, working in this other world, I do lose track of the feeling. However Zadore has brought it all back to me, and that is so wonderful.'

I liked the look in her shining eyes just then. I wanted to share the wonder too. 'Tell me some more about the Hopi beliefs,' I asked.

'Okay,' said Rose. 'I'll tell those parts which relate closest to Zadore's message for me. Maybe then you will appreciate them better.

'The Hopi have always seen the Sun as the well-head of all things. From the Sun emanate what might be called Dragons – Wind, Rain, Thunder, Light – and from these is the Earth brought forward, followed by all the creatures of the Earth. These Dragons are called the Potencies of the Powers.

They are not Gods, but are forces, and Creation is seen as being the Dragon's Den, or a vast sun furnace where all is forged into being. Men are also forged there. I suppose that the center of the Galaxy is like that furnace, and maybe every star. Whatever this really meant to the Old People of my race, to me it means that we are not merely creatures grown out of the Earth, but are born of something greater and perhaps unknowable.

'My people have always venerated the snake and the eagle. To them the eagle is a Sun Power, but the snake represents the darkest origins of Creation and the Earth Power. I'm sure you've heard of the Hopi Snake Dance where Dancers carry rattlesnakes in their mouths. They do this to show that man must submit to the great origin powers of his life, and conquer them. The snakes, which are conquered by the man who has overcome his fear, go back to the Earth, taking with them his message of tenderness, of request and of power. The snakes go back as rays of love to the heart of the first sun. They also go back as arrows shot straight by Man's courage, into the Earth's core, or heart. In the core of the first sun lies a poison as bitter as that of the rattlesnake, and this must be overcome. I wonder if this is the poison of Mankind's forgetting, for it is said that this poison is that which chains Man to the illusion of his Destiny. We Hopi believe that it is Man's duty to become aware, as one must be if one is to handle the snake without danger to oneself. Our awareness must travel always, back and forth between the darkest origins of creation to its brightest edifices, and having conquered the snakes within us, we are free to become a God. All these things, Jon, I have been taught from my childhood and the words of Zadore have opened them up for me again.'

'You're very fortunate to have so much inside you, Rose. My spiritual training seems arid and empty beside that. Have you ever handled a rattlesnake, though?'

Rose grinned. I think she was amused by my ignorance. 'Me? Heavens no! It is only the men who do that. It isn't considered necessary for women because it's reckoned that women already have access to the core and the power of Creation through their intimate relationship with birth and life.'

'That's interesting,' I said. 'Because I've often felt that men try to reserve the power of religion for themselves, and secret societies and brotherhoods and the like, because they feel powerless in the face of Mystery. And maybe women embody that Mystery naturally, and so men envy them that, and want a Mystery of their own.'

'You could be right. I hadn't thought of that,' said Rose. 'But are we not all embodying the mystery every day, although we may have forgotten that we do? Zadore has chosen you to carry his message to the world, and you are a man.'

Rose's statement of fact brought me back suddenly to the inadequacy I had been feeling since Zadore had dropped that bombshell on me. I had not told her how I felt about this, but now I really wanted to. Talking with Rose had become so reassuring. I felt I was not alone and that she would do what she could to support me.

I said: 'Listening to you, I think it should be you who takes the message from the Sun to the people of this planet. You have much more understanding than I. I don't think I'm the best person for the job, and I'm not even sure I want—'

With a wave of her fork she silenced me. 'Don't put yourself down like that! Of course you are the right person; Zadore knows what he's doing!'

I wondered how she could be so certain when I was not. 'You seem to be sure, Rose?'

'I am. I trust Zadore and I trust my own instinct,' she said vehemently. 'And don't say that you don't want to do it!' she added, with a force that surprised me.

I knew that anything I said after this would sound like lame excuses, but I said them anyway. 'Well, I've been worrying about how to do it. I'm no writer. I know nothing about publicity. I'm just a geologist. And then there is Carl and the intelligence agency. What if they were to get into the act? I've heard how people disappear when they're involved in secret cover-ups.'

'So that's what it is, you're afraid. You said you weren't,' said Rose, reproachfully.

Oh God, is that the truth? I thought. Am I just afraid for my own neck? So now I had another doubt to add to the rest. I didn't know how to answer her. Suddenly I felt very depressed.

In silence we looked at one another, and after what seemed like an uncomfortable eternity, while Rose speared me with a penetrating gaze, she spoke. 'No, you're not afraid, not of Carl or the secret service spooks anyway. But something worries you. What is it?'

I struggled with my thoughts and feelings but nothing seemed to want to come. I was saved then by Gloria with the coffee and after that we haggled over who was picking up the check. I wanted to, but Rose would not let me, so in the end we paid our share and I left the tip. In silence again we walked out into the night.

I believed that Rose was annoyed with me. We stopped by her car – I was parked a couple of spaces down – but she did not open her car door right away. Instead, she stood and looked at me with that gentle expression on her face.

'Jon, I'd like to help you. What's wrong? Please try to tell me.'

I shrugged. You have to come out of hiding sometime, so it might as well for someone who is kind. 'I don't know, Rose. I don't know if I can be what Zadore wants. He said I have to become the message, but how can I do that?'

'Do you think you're not good enough?'

I shrugged again.

'Jon,' said Rose. Then, quite surprising me, she reached out her hand and took mine. 'You don't see the Light in yourself – the power that you carry. But Zadore does, and so do I. This last transmission today made it plain how terribly important Zadore's mission is, so do you think he would have chosen you if you weren't the right one? He believes in you, Jon, and I believe in you too.'

She said this so sincerely and was such feeling that I had to hug her. And before I knew it I was kissing her too, and she made no objection but kissed me in return. When, reluctantly, we finally pulled apart, she raised her eyes to mine and smiled. Gently, she touched my cheek. 'Jon, we Hopi have a saying: "When the man learns to listen to his heart he has taken first step on the trail to freedom." I'll see you in the morning. I'll try to get there early.'

I sighed. 'So will I. Drive safely, Rose.'

Rose opened her car door. 'You too,' she said then quickly she turned to me. 'Oh, I just had a thought. Do you think it would be wise to copy the transmission tapes, in case Carl tries something underhanded?

In the dark, I blushed. 'I've already been doing that.' I fished out the latest transmission from my jacket pocket where I had slipped it when no one was looking. 'I was taking this home to do it. Zadore said I should.'

Rose nodded and smiled. 'See you tomorrow then.'

I drove home in a dream somewhat different from the one of Wednesday evening, for this time it was not my head that was in a whirl, but my heart. I could hardly believe what had happened this night. I felt like a teenager again, with passions stirring in me that I had not allowed myself to experience for many years.

When I got home I let my tape deck do its work while I whistled in the shower. Then, instead of sleeping, I listened to the voice of Zadore over and over as he spoke of the Illusion. Rose was right, I could not turn away from the role I was meant to play. It was all too important. Zadore's message had to become My Message, no matter what!

CHAPTER 9

The Entrapment

Friday morning arrived, and with it some of my doubt and uncertainty returned. Even to the extent that I was worried that Rose's tenderness towards me might have been the result of her kindness and friendship rather than what I wanted it to be. I had not forgotten her kisses of course, but in my unsure state I could tell myself anything. I could not help remembering that I was the one who had initiated the kisses, and perhaps she had just been swept away by the moment.

I was still worrying at the site office when Rose got there not long after I had. She walked through the door and she was glowing. I was sitting at my desk, shuffling distractedly through my work reports. 'What a lovely morning it is!' she said, and we shared a smile. Even across the room I could feel the energy bounce between us and Rose's warm glow penetrating straight into my heart. 'You look wonderful today, Rose,' I said.

'I feel wonderful, and it's all because of you,' she said, and came straight over to my side. Then she bent and kissed me on the lips.

How could I ever doubt what that meant? 'What an idiot I am!' I told myself joyously.

Before Carl arrived, we discussed what we ought to do about him. We could not exclude him from the transmission sessions, and, in any case, Zadore had specifically mentioned that all three of us were important to the Message. However he had not said in what way. So we decided that Carl was best left undisturbed while we two would keep our separate eyes on him. With Rose, Carl was more open, whereas I only seemed to antagonize him. If he said anything revealing it would be only to Rose. I realized and so did she that nothing of our altered relationship should communicate itself to Carl. This is going to be difficult, I thought, having to bury such wonderful feelings when all I want to do is express them.

Carl's car pulled up outside and we stiffened ourselves for his arrival. After the angry way he had retreated yesterday we were ready for anything – displays of temper, the sulks, bad feeling – anything.

But Carl was a chameleon. His face was its habitual bland self, his whole manner matter of fact and business-like. As if no capsule had ever existed, he offered us both his brief 'Good Morning', commented briskly on the weather, and sat down at his desk and organized his day's work.

What is he up to? I wondered. I saw that Rose was wondering, too.

We marched off to the trenches, and nothing changed. Nothing obvious, that is, for I thought I could detect a certain coldness in his attitude to me. He was rather more buddy-buddy with Rose however, and sat by her when we ate our lunch in the shade of some boulders nearby. I eavesdropped on their mumbled conversation, but heard nothing in Carl's half of it that was anything more than trivial or pertaining to the job. It was only when we were heading back to the office that I sensed another aspect to Carl. It was the impression that he was somehow pleased with himself. A queer look on his face when he glanced at me – a kind of smug self satisfaction – set me instantly on guard.

'Transmission time?' said Rose eagerly when we had tidied away our day's work.

Carl merely shrugged, as if he had ceased to care. Yet he stayed behind to hear it all the same.

'Okay,' I said, and unlocked the cabinet and took out the capsule and recorder. Out of the corner of my eye I caught one brief expression of dismay on Carl's impassive face, together with a slight shudder of his entire body then it was gone.

The transmission began:

ZADORE SPEAKS:

'It was time to commence the projection of a new wave of consciousness to the Earth. New body forms were implanted into the radiation belts and reflected once more to the Earth's consciousness. These forms were modified morphogenetic patterns that had not previously been manifested in the Third-dimension. They were able to accept greater energies and have the potential to carry the Earth to its ascension. To later members of the human race, it appeared that there was a missing link in the evolution of the species.

Soon the Earth prepared its bodies once more. The new patterns moved quickly through older patterns, on their way to the expression of the current form now seen on the planet and which you currently occupy. Soon they were ready to accept the higher consciousness that was beaming through the Sun. The Astrals looked on, and were shut off from being able to interfere with these new bodies. This angered them immensely, for although they duplicated the image of these new bodies on the etheric level of the Third-dimension, they were unable to maintain this form for any length of time, and when they approached these Earth bodies, their essence was repelled, for their polarity was incompatible. Seeing this, the Galactic Lords commenced the conscious seeding of the Earth bodies. And so it began.

87

What is important for your understanding now is that the Light Consciousness in that, which you call Man, is only a projection of consciousness from specific star systems that are working for the Earth's ascension. The current projections of consciousness are the same ones that commenced about 25,000 years ago. In other words, there has been no new seeding since that time. Why? Because the original projections of consciousness from the other systems in the Galaxy were trapped on this dimension, and that is what you will learn in this transmission.

The cradle of the new race was located on land masses which existed where much of the Pacific Ocean currently is. It was not called Lemuria, as this word was coined by scientific researchers in the late 19th Century. They called this civilization Lemuria because, on the Pacific islands, they found an ancient animal that was called Lemuroidea, which was similar to a monkey-ape. And, true to form, these researchers deduced that all human bodies are the result of evolution from prior species, so they decided that the ancient people of this continent were developed from that animal, and called the continent Lemuria.

The Earth bodies were called Mu, and the land was the land of Mu. Descendants of the people of Mu later became that race of people now called Atlanteans. Atlantis was a later civilization that occupied an island continent in the Atlantic Ocean. To understand this more easily, consider that about two thousand years ago in Europe there was the Roman Empire, which had reached a certain ascendancy over all other civilizations at that time. Now, some two thousand years later, that civilization does not exist, but currently we see that the United States of America on another continent holds the greatest power and achievements of the planet. So with the decline of Mu, Atlantis later became the major point of civilization at that time. It was a movement in time, not another seeding.

The various frequencies of Galactic Light moved harmoniously through space on the crystal rays that interconnect the Galaxy, as well as the Universe. They were stepped-down in frequency as they moved through the Sun, and once more as they entered the radiation belts of the Earth. It was here that they took on their first patterns of form, as they entered the higher levels of the Fourth-dimension. A second step-down occurred when they moved through the second radiation belt and entered the etheric level of the Third-dimension, and began to assume a denser form. It was at this level that the form was grounded in the Ego pattern, which was necessary for them to act and experience the Third-dimension in an Earth body.

For each individualized frequency of light consciousness an Energy Vortex forms on the lowest level of the Fourth-dimension, which spirals to the surface of the Earth, allowing the consciousness to mold with the baby form in the mother on the Earth. The Vortex is never far from the mother carrying the baby. This Vortex is called the Life Vortex, and it is grounded close to where the baby is born.

When the baby moves into the birth canal, simultaneously the Light Consciousness and the newly formed Ego move through the Life Vortex, and its entry into the Earth body coincides with the first breath of the baby. For the first time the Light Consciousness experiences both restriction and separation, plus the new experience of density and a sensual joy. Prior to the entry of the consciousness, the fetus is nurtured by the Elemental Beings, and one such Being continues to assist the cyclic maintenance of that body until the last breath is drawn.

At this point of time, the Light Consciousness begins to manifest on the Earth, nourishing and uplifting the Earth's consciousness as it is channeled back and forth through the many Life Vortices. The Third-dimension is the dimension of limitation, and the body and Life Vortex all have a time-span of manifestation before they break down. The Life Vortex lasts approximately one hundred and forty- four Earth years before it disintegrates. Currently on the planet, the average body lasts about seventy- five years. Some last longer, whilst others participate in shorter stays, however the Life Vortex still awaits its full time before disintegration at its original point of entry on the Earth.

During the conscious life cycle there is a constant flow of information that the Ego experiences from the five senses back through the Life Vortex, and a return flow or interpretation from the Light Essence on the Fourth-dimension. Much is also channeled back to the Sun, which monitors the Earth's evolvement and, when necessary, projects new morphogenetic patterns to the upper radiation belt for the greater development of the Ego-based beings. The voided Life Vortex, after it has been abandoned on the demise of the Earth body, is sometimes used by its previous disincarnate Ego, which for some reason or another did not want to leave the Third-dimension. That Ego becomes grounded close by where it died and attempts to continue its earthly life, only being noticed by sensitive individuals.

Often the Ego may remain trapped on the etheric level of the Third-dimension for hundreds of years.

THE ENTRAPMENT

Over many thousands of years, researchers have sought the location of the fabled Garden of Eden.

However, this garden is the Earth itself. As the Light Consciousness moved into the Earth bodies awaiting their incarnation, the Egos were receptive to the purpose and needs of the Light Consciousness. Thus the grand cycle of the Earth's ascension commenced. The Earth beings transformed the patterns of light and consciousness frequency into frequencies for the development of Earth's nature. It was in this loving fashion that the Earth began to blossom.

Watching from the Fourth-dimension, the Luciferian Astral Entities became dismayed, for they saw the transformation occurring, which, in time, would move the Earth into the Fifth-dimension, taking with it the Fourth-dimension which is currently their domain. They knew that they could not pass through the transformation and, as such, they would be cast into greater density, for they were not prepared to atone. Their pride could not allow them to seek forgiveness, for pride was the basis of their transgression. They were clever enough to understand fully how the sensual body of the Earth functioned, and the power of its separation on an earth-bound Ego.

The Earth bodies followed the normal cycles of the Third-dimension, in that at a particular point they deteriorated and the body returned to the Earth once more, and the Light Consciousness moved back to its Galactic Star. The Astrals, possessing the knowledge of the functions of the Earth bodies and its Egos, knew that they could entice the Ego to become more attached to the body and its senses, through creating sensual resonance with it.

It should be understood at this time that all information that the body receives is through a resonant action. When you feel something, the sense of touch harmonizes with the frequency of that which is felt. The frequency creates a tonal frequency that passes information in the form of feeling to the Ego. It either likes it or is repelled by it. However, all in all, information is received. On a higher level, the Light Consciousness moves frequencies to the Ego, setting up a resonant field that harmonizes with the Ego, which, in turn, passes this information into matter through the senses. In this way, the consciousness of the total Earth body receives greater information, which becomes part of the collective consciousness of the Earth.

The Astrals, using the same principles, moved their frequencies through to the Earth bodies. They began to plant in the dream-consciousness of the Earth Egos a frequency of power and domination over the Earth and all the Third-dimension. However, the Astrals could not directly influence the Earth Egos, but appealed to the taint already in the DNA that welled up as a memory of greatness. It appealed also to the principle of choice that exists in the Universe, for it was this principle which became the original downfall of the Astrals.

Thus, when the Egos of the Earth bodies turned their sight to the matter of the Third-dimension, they not only literally fell into matter, but, at the same time, enslaved their Light Essence, creating a virtual prison on the Fourth-dimension. They could no longer return to their Galactic Star home at the end of an incarnation in the Earth body. They blocked the passage of Light Consciousness to the Earth.

Now, having captured the Ego consciousness, the Astrals generated the Time Dimensional Loop whereby they could influence events to flow toward the same destructive completion ad infinitum. Much of this was covered in the last transmission; however, once the Illusion was ingrained into the consciousness of the Earth beings, who imagined that everything they saw and experienced was real and that the body they were conscious of was them, then the work of the Astrals was complete. They could manipulate these Earth consciousnesses at will to serve their own purpose, which had not changed over millennia. The longer the Astrals can maintain the Illusion, the more they prevent the Earth's ascension.

What the Astrals did not calculate at the beginning of their deception was that the dimensional loop, because it operates on the Third-dimension, shortens when it reaches its conclusion. For nothing can remain on the Third-dimension forever; it must move in cyclic fashion. It appears that many factors of the Earth's ascension and evolution are reaching a climax. The Illusion will begin to degenerate, and the Astrals are moving to have their demands met before it is too late for them and they are banished further into matter, with a lessening of power. For, over many years of rebirth and experience, the human consciousness has opened the frequencies of the Third-dimension to such a degree of sensitivity that the Astrals could be moved permanently onto the Third-dimension, as the Earth and its consciousness moves to the Fourth-dimensional consciousness. If this occurs, then the

Astrals will be moved into an existence of greater restriction and density.

This is the end of the transmission. More will follow.'

As the light from the capsule dimmed, Carl abruptly got up from his seat. 'It's late,' he said. 'I'm going home.'

'Goodbye, Carl,' said Rose.

'Well, what do you think of that?' she said to me after Carl's car had roared away.

'I'm not sure. But, quite obviously, he didn't want to talk. Has he said anything significant to you at all today?' I asked.

'Not a darned thing. It's pretty strange, don't you think?' I had to agree.

'Are you going to copy the transmission now?' asked Rose then. 'I'll make some coffee while you do, if you like.'

'That will be real fine, thanks,' I said. 'I record on hi-speed, so it doesn't take very long.' 'Great,' replied Rose. 'Because I have a little proposition to put to you when you're done.' Surprised, I grinned at her. 'A proposition? Now that sounds very interesting.'

She laughed. 'Not that kind of proposition!'

'Oh,' I said, and I have to admit that I was disappointed.

As we drank coffee she told me. For quite a while she had been longing to listen to the transmissions for a second time.

'Every night I've been going over them in my mind, but I always seem to have forgotten some of it,' she explained.

'You make me feel ashamed,' I confessed. 'I need to listen to them again, too – Zadore even chewed me out for not doing it – but there didn't seem to be the time and what with the worries about Carl.'

Rose nodded. 'I know … it's hard…' her dark eyes grew wide, 'Zadore chewed you out?' 'Yep. He said I had to study them – learn what was in them, if ever I wanted to become the message.'

Rose patted my hand. 'You have had a time of it, haven't you? But Zadore is right, it's the only way.

That's my proposition in any case. I thought we might do

something about it over the weekend, together.'

'You want to study them with me?'

'That's the idea. We both need to hear them again and, if I'm going to help you, I'll have to.'

'You want to help me in this?' I was beginning to sound like a broken record. 'You are with me in this?'

'All the way,' said Rose. 'After last night I thought you would have realized that.' She gazed at me intently, then a sudden look of doubt swept across her face and she took her hand away. 'That is…if… if you want me to.'

I drew back her hand and held it closely. 'Oh, Rose. Yes, I want!'

We made plans for the weekend – Rose was to come over to my apartment at about eleven the next morning and stay over. Her place, she said, was far too small and the neighbors far too nosy. Of course, I liked the idea of her staying. My apartment was quite spacious – in fact, I tended to rattle around in it a bit – and it overlooked the beach. Rose was very fond of the beach. She told me of a beach-house that one of her more well-heeled aunts owned. It was a vacation place just out of San Diego and over the years she had spent several months vacationing there on college breaks and in between jobs.

So off we both went to our respective homes, looking forward to the next two days. I grabbed something to eat on the way because I knew I would have to do some straightening up of the apartment before the morning. I am not the tidiest of guys, although I am not a slob, but I usually tossed all my clean laundry on the bed in the spare room before I got stuck into it with the iron, and I wanted this room to look its best for a guest as nice as Rose.

Then I decided that the whole place needed a general going

over – a task I usually raced through on Saturday morning along with the grocery shopping. I spent the next two hours like a frantic charlady, until I was certain that Rose would be impressed, and I was worn out and ready to crash.

But instead of crashing I sat for a while by my living room window and stared at the moon shining over the water. The moon was quite large and very bright, but it was not yet full. Not quite a Lover's Moon, I reflected dreamily. My thoughts wandered then to the capsule and the tapes. I knew I could not wait until the transmissions were over before I had worked out a plan regarding them. No matter what Carl's objections might be, the capsule would be returned to the place where I had found it, and I knew it would be capable of looking after itself. The tapes were a worry, though. Although there were copies, I realized that they would have to be put in safe-keeping, in a place separate from the originals, as I did not want Carl getting his hands on both. I had no idea what he would try, but I was fairly certain he would try something.

Finally I decided to leave the problem until tomorrow – I was too tired to think any more – and made one last inspection check of the spare room.

Sure, it passed muster. Actually it was spotless. I put out the light, then realized I had not closed the drapes. Like the master bedroom, this second room had a lovely view of the ocean, but it also had a small window which partly overlooked the street. There was a street light opposite, illuminating a section of the road and sidewalk, and in the half shadow by a wall I thought I saw someone loitering.

The figure moved then, only slightly, but enough into the light so that I could see it better. It was a man; a strange looking character dressed totally in black with a broad black hat something like Hasidic Jews wear. The strange figure then tilted back his head and stared across the road and, so I felt, stared straight at me.

Involuntarily I shuddered. Eyes which I could not see were staring into mine! No – I would not believe it. No one could see me at the darkened window. Yet, foolishly, I felt like drawing back.

Resisting the impulse to flee, and though it caused me some real unease, I stayed to watch. The man did not move – I am sure to this day that he did not – however in the blink of an eye he disappeared – he simply vanished in front of me!

Shaking a little, I closed the drapes and hurried out of the room. By then I was telling myself that my eyes were playing tricks. Nevertheless I needed a shot or two of good old Jack Daniels before I felt ready for bed.

CHAPTER 10

Vortex

Saturday morning and, damn it all, I woke up very late. I had been having some weird, awful dream, which, thankfully, I promptly forgot right away. I didn't take time for breakfast but raced like a madman to the stores for groceries and a nice bottle of wine. I intended to concoct a really good meal for Rose that night, because actually, even if I say so myself, cooking is one of my pleasures and I am pretty good at it.

Back at my car I was about to drive off when I noticed a striking window display in a flower shop nearby. That was the final touch I needed. I dashed into the shop and bought two bunches of beautiful roses, one of red and one of white. They were still in bud, not quite ready to open, but the sales clerk assured me that by the evening they would begin to unfold and spread their lovely perfume everywhere.

I could not get over the excitement I felt, but it was not just because Rose was coming to stay. It was the transmissions too, and the thought that we could begin to study them in depth. Somehow, I believed, just listening to them again would stir in me a greater awakening, and having Rose there, to bounce my feelings off and to know hers, would help a lot. Rose herself had managed to stir me in several ways, not the least being the physical. But that is not as crass as it might sound. Awakenings come in many forms, and mine were uniting towards one thrilling end. As I learned from Zadore, we are not made of little separate parcels, such as a body, an intellect, a set of emotions, or a bunch of fizzing chemicals. We are not an Ego either, or a soul, as some have expressed it. We are more like a great, wonderful wave of Light, that encompasses everything, and for what we are about here on this Earth that 'everything we are' must flow in harmony, without obstruction. As I said before, I had been denying my heart – my feeling self – for too long a time, and that was restricting my flow of Light.

Well, it was Rose who had helped to awaken this in me, and the fact was thrilling me from head to toe.

I did not give Rose the flowers when she arrived. The red ones, I had set in a vase in the spare room for a welcome gift, and the white I had decided to keep for the dinner table later. When she saw the red roses she seemed surprised, but pleased. 'No one has ever given me flowers before,' she said, and thanked me. 'Roses for a lovelier Rose,' I said. I knew it sounded corny but I really meant it.

I guess that, by now, Rose had reckoned me a hopeless romantic, for she gave me the strangest smile I ever saw. It was as if there was some secret behind that smile and she was not telling anyone what it was.

Even though that weekend was the best I had spent in my life up until then, I will not go into great detail about it. I must mention though that I did not tell Rose of my unnerving experience on Friday night – I saw no reason to worry her about things that may have been only imagined by a tired brain.

Nevertheless, I will write about some of the most important events in consciousness during those two special days, and which Rose and I both shared.

All day Saturday we listened to the transmissions, only breaking for lunch and an occasional coffee, so by dinner time we were filled to overflowing with information and ideas and we were fairly tired. We had not merely listened passively, but in between tapes had gotten into long discussions and expressions of feelings that, although exciting and stimulating, kind of drained us both. Even while I cooked the meal – I don't let guests cook their own dinner – Rose hovered by the kitchen bench and we brain-stormed one another.

So we decided to call a halt and enjoy our dinner in peace. I put the white roses on the table and Rose grinned and shook her head at me as if to say I was incorrigible. Then we really did enjoy that meal and, afterward, a little pleasurable relaxation. As I retired that night I came to realize how lonely I had made myself for the last ten years. It is strange and stupid how we can inure ourselves to emptiness and stagnation, so that we hardly notice that our lives are hollow and at a virtual standstill.

On Sunday morning, during a somewhat late breakfast, Rose said to me: 'I don't think I can take any more of the intellectual stuff today. What say we just listen and let the whole thing wash over us, then see what happens.'

Willingly I agreed. I had been feeling much the same way myself.

And that is what we did. Also we did not listen to the tapes in their chronological order, but let each other choose the parts we wanted to hear.

'Could we have Thursday night's transmission?' asked Rose. 'I'd like to hear that bit about the Illusion again.'

'Just that bit, or the whole transmission?'

'Oh, you might as well begin at the beginning.'

I found the tape and started it going and we both sat back and closed our eyes. I was seated in my favorite chair and Rose had gravitated from the sofa to a floor cushion against the wall. The white roses, I had placed on the coffee table between us and, true to the sales clerk's word, they had gradually opened and the room was filled with their glorious, almost overpowering scent.

As I moved into the words of the transmission, it seemed that I was moving into the heart of the Sun itself. But not the Sun as we see it from Earth. Rather, it was the Sun of Zadore, with Zadore's words coming to me from inside my own mind and opening a gateway there – a gateway rimmed with an incandescence, which poured from the worlds I could see through it. And, opening within that was a form of a great Eye, which seemed to be gazing into my heart and mind. I gazed back, in wonder and in love. Was this Zadore?

Then it was that the Eye grew even larger and I passed through its portal and flew on invisible wings into a Sea of Being where everything flowed into everything else. Then on and down, where the world spun in light and a vortex of living energy.

Into the vortex, I plunged. Into the deep, unutterable wonder, I danced and flew with radiant Beings of Light – the Elemental Beings who plunge into the heart of the glorious Earth and ride the rainbows into rock and flower and every living creature, to work their magic of integrity and renewal.

It was all glorious and selfless – a radiant descent of love, which I too experienced in my ecstasy.

I reveled in the Moving Spirit of Being in Nature. Everything flowed in me, and I in it – or, as I should say, I was not separate from the flow of Being, but was the flow itself. Being was me, I was Being. I experienced the livingness of the trees, or the Standing People, as the American Indians so fitly call them. I poured through the holes in the Earth and entered its crystal heart. I felt the Earth Mother's currents, energies, as a magical tingling in my spine, (even while I seemed to float apart from the body at this time). I felt as if I was a huge tree – an ancient Redwood maybe – as up my spine — whoosh! the flow of life energy poured. And shot out through the branches of my skull, until my body seemed alive with a wonderful fire. A flower blossomed in my heart, and one deep inside the center of my head. They poured their power upwards like a fountain, and I poured with it. It was the fireworks display of all time!

Then up and out again. The eyes of my consciousness belonged to the Sun. Was I Zadore? I dwelt in the Sun, but was not of the Sun. I passed the Sun's portal through me, as if I was the Gateway it shined through, and which channeled its Being with mine to a greater Source.

And while in the Sun I saw the sorrowing of the Light as it was separated from the lower dimensions in the Illusion created by the lower Astral frequencies. Into this Illusion I plunged, falling deeper and deeper, fearing that I would be lost. But, of course, I could not be lost, as I was seeing ALL and being ALL in my awakened state.

But I felt the pain – knowing the agony of separation – yet I knew also that it had its purpose. I felt the frailty of this human dilemma, that the Illusion's existence rested on a precarious point of balance, which relied upon the human consciousness only turning itself in one direction. The Astrals had invented a House of Cards, that, with the right impulse from us all, could topple and disappear. If only we would turn our faces from their parody of life, then would the pain cease to exist.

Oh, suffering world – my heart cried for it. Oh, fatuous Ego – frail yet buoyed by the power of aeons of assertion and fighting for a separation that only caused it pain, when all it needed was to surrender itself in unconditional love to its Source.

Then briefly did I view the ghastly specter of an evil which had no substance, unless I gave it credence and allowed it to enter my consciousness. It reared up before me like a threat, bearing Carl's imagery of Razparil and challenging me, with a sort of ghastly, superhuman arrogance and pride, to be more than It was. But it had no place in my ecstasy. It seemed a vapid frailty, empty though so pompous that, in my Sun Consciousness, I laughed and turned away.

Yet I was drifting back into an everyday consciousness again. The accustomed separateness struggled to assert itself, and although I protested, I let it come. Sorrow entered me, but joy and elation, too. Sorrow because I knew that this vision had not yet fulfilled itself in me. Joy and elation because I knew it would.

My mind filled with the spirit-tears of all these emotions at once, and then my physical eyes followed. Blinking back the salt, I opened my eyes. To see Rose with her eyes closed and as still as one of the flowers on the coffee table, with tears streaming down her cheeks. Her long dark hair framed the beautiful oval of her face in such a way that she looked like a sorrowing madonna – all alight with love and glory, but bowed also with the sadness of the world. Then she opened her eyes and gazed at me from pools of shining, wet obsidian, and I knew that she was in joy from an experience of her own.

I scrambled over to her – I could not keep away – and took her in my arms. She lay her head on my chest and held me too, and we stayed that way – silent and sharing energies – for possibly half an hour. It was the sweetest half hour of my life.

That charmed space between Friday night and Sunday HAD to come to an end, and though I would have liked it to go on forever, the inevitable work day was soon on my doorstep.

It was going to be a hot one, I thought, as I dodged through the tedious traffic of LA. Once out of the city congestion and on the out-bound route, I took time to reflect on the possibilities for the day. I wondered how Carl might be doing. What game was he going to play this time? And I thought about Rose for the umpteenth time. It had only been twelve hours since I had seen her, but already it seemed too long.

I pondered the transmission, too, asking myself how many more there might be. Between us, Rose and I had decided that it would be best to secure the tapes in a bank safety deposit box, or something like that, once they were done.

Our work day was not unusual or eventful, and Carl seemed to be continuing with his farcical game of Friday. To stifle our enthusiasm for each other, Rose and I concentrated very hard on measuring layers and making meticulous notes. I worried that we might be trying just too darn hard, and that Carl would get wind of us, however he did not appear to notice anything unusual in our behavior.

At 4.00 P.M. we were back at the site office and glad of it too, because the day was a scorcher. We tidied up and I got out the capsule. It was like a ritual we had become trained to perform by now. We sat down – Carl without any comment – to wait for the session to begin, and when it did, it came as a shock.

ZADORE SPEAKS:

'This is the last transmission from this light capsule. After this message is completed you must return it to the place where you first found it, for it is to be returned to the source from whence it came. Remember the message and teach it to others who are waiting at this time for their return to their system in the Galaxy. The moment is fast approaching when there will be no return of the Inter- dimensional loop, so it is a time of decision not only for the Humans but also for the Astrals. The Earth can wait no longer. Its time of transformation is near.

There has been for some while now an increasing number of time-travelers in the ethers surrounding the planet Earth. These travelers are from various star systems and dimensions in this Galaxy. They are using Third and Fourth-dimensional craft; however there are others from higher dimensions who are here to witness the change.

Often, those travelers of Third-dimensional realms of other star systems have penetrated the atmosphere of the planet Earth. They cannot stay long because they are Third-dimensionally oriented to different environmental gases than those of the Earth, so their penetration is only of a short duration. They know that Fifth-dimensional consciousnesses from their star systems are trapped in human bodies, and they attempt to abduct those of their own kind who are in the human body. They hope that through such abductions they can somehow capture the Fifth-dimensional consciousness for their own advancement, for they too, as Third-dimensional frequencies, are subject to the same laws of the Cosmos as the Ego of the Earth body consciousness. However, their abductions never accomplish anything, as they only penetrate the Earthly consciousness, which is currently ignorant of its higher Light, and the abduction increases fear in those abducted, when they are returned to the Earth environment. These interfering beings are only increasing their karma and becoming more trapped in the galactic Third-dimension.

Fourth-dimensional beings from other star systems are also

103

attempting to manifest their presence, through dreams, to those of their star systems, in a similar way to the Astrals. They are here to witness the ascension of the Earth, as well as of those Fifth-dimensional entities who have been trapped for so long. These Fourth-dimensional beings attempt to move into the Earth consciousness by channeling or walk-in methods. This has always been the prerogative of the Astrals, so planetary life is becoming quite confusing. It is out of this confusion that change will occur.

The great purpose of my consciousness being now focused to Planet Earth is to send forth the great Vortex of Light and Healing. This Vortex will be freely available to all those who are awaiting release and freedom from all restrictions, from the wheel of rebirth, from Astral control, from all the darkness and fear that had been beamed across the planet. The Vortex will allow those waiting, to turn and face their own Light, and surrender their Ego to the service of the Great Light, and re-focus Light to the Earth's ascension.(8) They will then return to their star systems as beings with a Light Body that will become co-creators of the Universes. During the process of personal transformation, they will add Light and Power to the Vortex, which will progressively draw more and more to their own freedom and, in so doing, will free the Earth of the evil, destructive elements working for its destruction. Not all Earth beings will return to the Light, for some have become as Astrals themselves and, as such, will be doomed to the fate of these elements. Everything that exists is of Light, and, in due course, all will return to Light. Some will become Light Beings in the font of Light. Your choice is here ... NOW.

My teachings on the Vortex will be heard on Earth and will inspire those who are ready to reveal it to others, in writing, in color and in sound. My love to all beings, as we are all ONE in LIGHT.'

END OF THE FINAL TRANSMISSION.

CHAPTER 11

Betrayal

The capsule ceased transmission and there was utter silence in the room. I think we were stunned by the sudden climax of so many intense days and felt a little lost, perhaps. Although I had been expecting an ending soon, I could barely believe that this was the last time. But there it was – our contact with the capsule was over, for good.

No one said anything for a while. Carl seemed to have turned to stone. Rose was seated very still, with her hands folded in her lap, Then, only with her eyes, she looked up and gave me a questioning glance. I nodded very slightly. It was time; I could not put it off any longer.

I stood up. 'Well, I guess I have to make the hike back out to the trenches,' I said. I did not fancy another hot walk, but it had to be done. The capsule had to be returned.

Hastily Carl jumped to his feet. 'What are you going to do?'

'I'm taking the capsule back to where I found it.'

Carl stared at me, as if he believed I was insane. 'Why?'

'Have you forgotten Zadore's instructions?' I asked him. 'The capsule is set to self-destruct, so we have to get rid of it. We don't know what could happen if we kept it. It might be dangerous.'

'No, no.' Carl shook his head. 'I'm sure if we kept it in some sort of controlled environment, out of the weather, out of the air. That's it! We could set it up in a lab in town, in a vacuum chamber. That would prevent—'

I cut him off. 'I'm sorry, Carl, it has to go back. That was the deal, and I'm sticking to it.'

In disbelief Carl turned to Rose. 'Rose, you talk some sense into him! This is crazy! We need the capsule for scientific investigation and for verification. How will anyone believe us with just those tapes? They will think we made it all up!'

Rose started to answer, 'But Zadore wanted—' however Carl interrupted. 'You can't let him, Rose.

Think of your career, how great this thing could be for that. Think of what it could do for us all!' Well, you have the photographs you took,' said Rose, in reply. 'Won't they help verify everything?'

'Yes, I got photographs,' said Carl bitterly. 'But nothing was on them. All that came out was a blur of light.'

If matters had not been so tense I would have laughed then. However, I could see that Carl was in no mood for either laughter or reason. A decisive move had to be made, so I picked up the capsule and headed for the door. 'I'm going now. Sorry, Carl, but we have no choice.'

'OH, YES WE DO!'

Carl's face twisted in anger and he made a rush for me, but fortunately I was able to dodge out of his way in time. He banged heavily into the door frame, then leaned against it, rubbing his shoulder where he must have hurt it, and trembling.

I did not like the look in his eyes. I had not expected violence like this and I was trembling as well and hoping that it did not show. But I was a whole lot bigger than Carl. 'Look here, don't you start anything you may regret,' I said, with as much menace as I could muster.

I think Rose believed that we were going to get into a fight, for she rushed over and planted herself between us.

'Please, Carl, don't be so upset. Jon is doing what he thinks is right, he's not just trying to go against you. Please understand.'

Somehow her words seemed to calm Carl down. With a glare at both of us he slunk off to his desk and crouched in his chair. 'Have it your own way then. You're both crazy.'

Of course, I would not leave until I was sure that Rose would be safe alone with Carl. And with all that had happened, I had forgotten temporarily about the tape in the machine. Now I remembered. I took my keys and locked it in the cupboard with the others.

Carl was watching me closely. There was a bitter, angry expression on his face. 'What are you going to do with those then? Keep them all for yourself?' he said with a sneer and a sideways glance at Rose. Perhaps he thought he could make her his ally with suggestions that I would cheat them both.

'Don't be ridiculous,' said Rose. 'Jon would never do anything like that.'

Carl ignored her. 'We should all have a copy of those tapes. They're not just yours, you know.' 'I know,' I replied. 'I'll make copies if you want.'

Carl looked triumphant. 'Good. We can start on it now then. I'm not going home until I get them.' Luckily, there were no spare tapes in the office – we had used the last one, and I told him so.

Of course he refused to believe me and made a great fuss of turning the whole place over, in search. When he realized I was telling the truth, he seemed to sag suddenly and shrivel, as if the life had been let out of him.

'Why don't you just go home and get some rest,' I suggested to him. 'I'll be as quick as I can,' I told Rose. 'Then we can all go home.'

Carl went to his desk and picked up his car keys. They must

have sparked an idea, for quickly he said to me, 'How can I trust you, after all this? Give Rose the file cabinet key, so we can be sure that the tapes won't vanish. Then I'll go.'

'Okay.' I flicked the key off my ring and handed it to Rose. Seeming satisfied with that, Carl wandered out to his car and drove off.

'Obviously he still trusts you, at least,' I remarked to Rose as Carl vanished in a cloud of dust. 'He worries me,' she said, 'and I certainly don't trust him.'

'No, neither do I.' I gave her a quick kiss. 'Will you wait for me?'

'Sure. I hadn't planned on leaving the office till you got back, in case Carl decided to double back.'

That possibility had not crossed my mind, although it ought to have. However, this raised in my mind another disturbing idea. 'Go inside and bolt the door then,' I told her. 'Don't let anyone in but me.'

'Okay,' Rose agreed, although she looked puzzled by my order. 'Who would bother, besides Carl?' 'I'm just being careful,' I explained. 'Who knows who might be wandering around this area, and I don't want you alone and unprotected.'

I guess Rose must have thought me over-protective and rather old fashioned. Young women nowadays are less inclined to thank men for such attitudes. She did not argue the point; however she grinned at me wryly. 'You be careful yourself then,' she said.

I hurried off as fast as I could. Rose did not understand, of course, because I had not told her what was really worrying me. An image of a strange figure in black had jumped into my head and in spite of the fact that I told myself how foolish I was being, that image would not go away.

I reached the work site in double quick time and located the exact spot where the capsule had been.

Although the soil was already loose from the work I had done before, I was sweating as I dug a shallow trench out with my hands.

Feeling the need to hurry, I deposited the capsule quickly in the hole and covered it up with dirt. It seemed a hasty, most unceremonious ending for such a momentous and impressive object. I gazed briefly towards the Sun and thought of Zadore. My emotions were all mixed up. Then, in my solar plexus I felt a twinge of fear.

Hurrying back, I was relieved to find Rose alone and unperturbed, so I said nothing. We had made no plans for the evening and Rose said she was feeling rather tired. I suppose that was because of the conflict with Carl. So we agreed to go our separate ways and get some rest. Rose left and I stayed a while to re-record the last and final transmission. Then I too went home.

I had decided on an early night for once and was just getting ready for bed when the telephone rang.

I answered reluctantly, and it was Rose. She sounded agitated.

'Jon, sorry to bother you, but I had to call. I don't know why...intuition I suppose...but I had a strong feeling that something was wrong at the office.'

'Like what? What could be wrong?' I asked.

'That's just the point; I asked myself the same question. I just couldn't figure the feeling out, but it wouldn't go away, so, in desperation I drove all the way out—'

'You're at the office?'

'Yes, and my feeling was right; the office has been broken into. The file cabinet has been battered open and the tapes are gone!'

'CARL!' was all I could say at first, when another idea occurred. 'Do you think he went after the capsule as well? Is there any sign of him now?' I asked Rose.

'He probably did, and no, his car is not here,' she answered. 'Jon, what shall we do?'

Frantically I tried to think. 'Well, first of all you get out of there and back home, just in case. I'm going to drive over to

Carl's house and sort this out. That is if he's there.'

'I want to come too,' said Rose.

'I don't think that's a good idea. You go home and wait till I call you,' I replied.

Even over the phone I could feel Rose's indignation. 'Where I'm safe, you mean? Jon Whistler don't you—' she began; but I hung up in her ear. I guessed she would be pretty mad at me for that, but there was no way I wanted her at Carl's place if there was going to be trouble. As I changed back into my clothes I comforted myself with the thought that Rose had no idea of Carl's address.

The street was in one of those well-heeled, classy neighborhoods where there are fairly big homes with large, walled gardens. Not the ritziest spot in LA, but not bad for a working geologist's salary, I thought. I wondered how Carl managed the rent; it certainly would have been beyond me.

His house was 1135, at the darker end of the street where a lot of leafy shrubs grew tall around the streetlights. The lights were Twentieth Century made historical replicas, and not very high. I drove slowly down the road, counting the illuminated numbers on the walls until I found Carl's, then I drove a little further, about three or four houses on, where I parked on the opposite side of the street. If Carl was up to mischief with the capsule then, I wanted to catch him at it and not let him hear me coming.

As I stepped out of my car, another car slid by me and I immediately recognized whose it was. 'ROSE?' I muttered to myself.

Rose parked her car a little way from mine and hurried over. 'Thought you'd keep me out of this, did you?' she said.

'How do you know where Carl lives?' I asked.

Rose threw me a look of triumph. 'His address is on his file in the computer, don't forget.'

I sighed. She was way too sharp for me. 'You got here mighty fast,' I commented as we hurried down the sidewalk.

'Yes. The traffic was light coming in. You got here later than I thought you would, though.' 'Opposite reason,' I explained.

There was a light on in Carl's house; we could see it from his gate. While we were heading up the drive I began to think that it was a very peculiar kind of light – a strange blue light.

'The capsule!' We said it together. Rose gasped. 'How did he activate it?'

We ran to the front door and Rose rang the door bell. No one came to the door, so we figured he must be ignoring us. I banged and called out a couple of times, but there was no answer. Then, coming from inside, we heard a strange sound like an animal in pain. We hurried in the direction of the sound, to a window that was, luckily, undraped.

Through the window we saw Carl. He was laying on the floor with the tapes strewn all around him.

The capsule was in front of him and it was not only glowing, but a beam of light was passing from it into his forehead.

'NO! NO! I don't want to see that again! Once in a life is enough!'

Rose grasped my arm. 'He's reliving his life, he's going to die! We've got to help him!'

Carl seemed to be going into convulsions. His head was clasped in his hands as he rolled around the floor. We could hear his awful groaning cries. 'Somehow we have to get inside,' I said. However, as I said it, I saw that the capsule was beginning to melt. 'You cannot help him. Get out of here,' an inward voice ordered me.

I grabbed hold of Rose and we took off down the drive at top speed. At the gate we paused to catch our breath and stare towards the house. We couldn't believe what we saw. A light so bright that it hurt to look at it was pouring from the windows. I hurried Rose and myself out of the gate and down the street. There was no way I wanted to be around when the neighborhood woke up to what was happening at Number 1135!

We were out of the street and a couple of blocks away when

Rose suddenly pulled into the curb. I was following and over-shot, so I pulled over quickly and got out of my car. Rose was out of hers and running towards me, waving her arms at the sky. It was plain to see what excited her, for the whole sky above Carl's street was glowing. Then, up into the glow shot a ball of fiery light so dazzling, that even where we stood, two streets away, the night was turned into day. People began to pour out from the homes around us and I wondered how Carl's immediate neighborhood must be handling this sudden display of fireworks.

Rose put her hands to her distraught face. 'Oh, God, there's no way Carl could survive that! I hope no one else has gotten hurt, too.'

I placed my arm around her shoulders and held her reassuringly, although, to tell the truth, I wasn't so reassured myself. 'I don't think Zadore would allow that,' I said.

'Oh, look!' shouted a spectator standing nearby. The fiery ball had vanished, as if suddenly vaporized, and all that was left to light the night sky was the duller glow of an ordinary house fire. The wailing of fire trucks could be heard above the agitated conversations of the gathering in the street.

'Come on, there's nothing we can do,' I said to Rose calmly. I could see she was very upset and I wanted away from there myself. 'Get into your car and drive to my place. Okay?'

Mutely Rose nodded. I hoped she would be all right and would keep her mind on her driving, to get home safely before the awful reality of the situation set in.

'Oh, why did he do it?' exclaimed Rose in dismay.

'He seemed obsessed with the capsule, with keeping it. Maybe he was under instructions to get it,' I observed.

'Is he dead, do you think? Perhaps he could have gotten away?'

I shrugged. 'I doubt it. He didn't look in very good condition when we saw him.' 'We should have done something,' said Rose reproachfully.

I studied her unhappy face. I felt as distressed as she, but inwardly there was that voice again telling me that Carl's particular destiny was not ours to decide.

'You mustn't blame yourself,' I counseled. 'Carl knew that the capsule might be dangerous, and made his choice.'

Rubbing her hand across her forehead, Rose sighed deeply. 'You're right, I know. How did he activate the capsule, though?'

'Perhaps he didn't. Perhaps Zadore activated it.'

Incredulous, Rose stared at me. 'What? To contact Carl then to blow him up?

Put like that, it did sound rather brutal. Nevertheless, intuition told me that this was the truth.

'No, not just to blow him up. Carl had major problems, didn't he, and his only hope was to get free of the pact his father made in his name. Maybe there was only one way it could be done.'

'So dying was the only way?'

'And facing that awful vision of his life beforehand, so that he could willingly turn from his father's influence. I'm saying this because I'm remembering something that Zadore said when he spoke to me privately. He said the transmissions marked a turning point for Carl, and that he would find his own Light in time.'

Rose looked much more at peace then. 'If this is so then we shouldn't be sad for Carl, should we. I mean, death is not the worst thing, after a life like that.' Passionately she took my hands. 'Oh, Jon, there are so many suffering people. I will be glad to see this world change. And I'm glad I can be a part of doing something about it. We need an end to all the blindness and the slavery.'

I couldn't agree more. 'Amen to that,' I said.

CHAPTER 12

Intrigue

Following the tragedy of Carl I spent a wretched night punctuated by disturbing dreams and constant waking and listening for I knew not what. So that the dawn came as a relief, in spite of the fact that it was early and I did not feel like getting up.

I had asked Rose to stay with me and, after some persuasion, she did. Because she was so plainly upset by what had happened to Carl, I had not wanted her driving home to a lonely apartment. I was glad she decided to stay. To tell the truth, I felt better myself to be in company at such a time.

By 7.30A.M. I could lay in bed no longer. I looked in on Rose, but she seemed fast asleep, so I showered and dressed and, leaving a note on the refrigerator to tell her that I had to run an errand, I drove to the nearest news-stand. I wanted to see if the fire at Carl's had made it into the morning news and, if so, what details were known.

Rose was poking around my kitchen cupboards when I returned. 'I hope you don't mind, I thought I'd start some breakfast. Are you hungry?' she asked.

'Yes, I am a bit. Well, you look to have recovered from last night,' I commented.

Rose's expression was non-committal. 'I'm okay, I guess. I didn't sleep much. I seemed to spend a lot of the night chewing everything over and over, but, in the end, I think I managed some acceptance. If only I knew what really happened to Carl.'

I showed her the newspaper. 'Maybe there's something in here that will help.' We discovered an item in the Late News:

MAN DIES IN MYSTERY EXPLOSION

A man died and a house in Westwood was destroyed last night in an explosion that rocked an entire neighborhood. Witnesses say the explosion sent a fireball into the sky, turning night into day for residents several blocks away. The cause of the explosion is not known and police are investigating.

Interestingly, while the house was blown apart and entirely gutted in the ensuing fire, neighboring properties were undamaged. The dead man, Carl Reisenger, 49, a geologist working for the USGS, was the owner and sole occupier. Neighbors report him as a quiet man who kept to himself.

'That didn't tell us much,' said Rose. 'But at least nobody else got hurt.'

'The cops are investigating, though. I suppose we will have a visit from them when Head Office tells them where Carl was working.'

Rose grimaced. 'Oh, yes. What are we going to say, Jon? I will feel like a criminal even though I didn't do anything wrong. I hope no one noticed our cars or could identify the plates. Or us!'

We were just plain lucky I guess.

In spite of Rose's fears we never became suspects in the mystery of Carl Reisenger's death. The police were unable to find any cause or motive for the incident and none of the witnesses proved helpful. Arson was ruled out for lack of evidence and, finally, the explosion was labeled not as a crime but as one more unexplained accident to add to the long list that the over-worked Police Department had no time to bother with. The police did ask me if Carl had been interested in explosives, and I truthfully said I didn't think he was, but that I didn't know for sure, so it appears that they may have suspected him of playing with bombs in his own time. Perhaps they thought that he belonged to one of the Militia, because his reclusive nature was commented on during the interview. A man who keeps solely to himself is always bound to be suspected of something in this paranoid society of ours.

There was really only one anxious moment, I remember. On the Tuesday morning following the accident, after I had contacted Head Office, my boss, Alan Curtis told me that Rose and I had better not work that day but that I had to go out to the site because the police wanted to search for anything which might give a clue to Carl's behavior. That gave Rose and me quite a stir, because we suddenly remembered the battered file cabinet, and we did not have a clue what to do about it. Worrying about what I ought to say, we certainly did begin to feel something like criminals then.

However, a strange kind of luck seemed to be following me around. I had to ride with the police, since they had no idea where the site office was and it was off the highway and down a dirt track. I rode all the way in a sweat, feeling guiltier with every mile, but when we got to the office there was no sign at all of any break-in or damage! 'Rose can't have gotten it wrong?' I asked myself.

'Which is Reisenger's desk?' asked the investigating officer, and ignoring a clearly un-battered file cabinet.

'That one.' I pointed and he began to rummage through Carl's papers. I edged myself nearer the cabinet. How Rose could have imagined that it was damaged, I couldn't understand. Then I saw the truth. It was not the original cabinet but one so very like that, had I not looked closely, I would never have known.

'You got a box for these?' 'Er, yes.'

I found the officer a cardboard box and he began stuffing the papers into it.

'A lot of our research work will be in that,' I said. 'What's going to happen to it?'

'You'll get a receipt,' said the officer curtly. 'You'll get the stuff back when we've finished our investigation.' He cleared out Carl's desk completely, then slowly surveyed the room. His eyes lit on the cabinet. 'What's in there?'

As nonchalantly as I could, I shrugged. 'Nothing much. We use it for samples mainly, and small equipment.'

'I'll have it open,' the officer ordered.

I did a double take. My key would never fit the lock, I knew. What would I do now? The officer must have noticed my hesitation. 'What's the problem?' he asked.

'No problem,' I said quickly, in the feverish hope that a miracle would make it open, or if that failed I would be able to fob him off with some excuse of a lost key, I tugged at the handle and, WOULD YOU BELIEVE IT, it opened!

He pulled out the drawers and stuck his nose in each one, pulling back sharply from a couple. 'Phew! What's that stink?' he said.

'A delicate-nosed detective,' I joked to myself silently. By now I was feeling almost hysterically over-confident, like a gambler who can't believe his winning streak. 'That's the smell of dry peat,' I told him. 'I find it rather pleasant myself. You see, we use it to date earthquake—'

'Yeah, yeah.' He was not interested, and soon we were heading back to town.

Collecting my car from the car park at the precinct, I thought I would drive over to see Rose. She had gone home early so as to be there when the police arrived. She had also taken the transmission tapes with her because we had decided to make another set of copies, since the first was now destroyed. Carl may have been out of our lives, however we could not be sure who might take his place if keeping the tapes from publication was of such prime importance to the Astral Entities. A worrying idea, and reason enough to be extra careful.

'Have the cops been?' was the first thing I asked Rose.

'Yes. They didn't stay long either. How did you go at the site?' she asked anxiously. 'I've been worrying about you.'

'That's nice,' I said. I was still a little high on my luck. 'It was a bit hairy, and also very strange.

Will you believe me when I tell you that someone else has been there overnight and fixed everything up? We even have a new file cabinet, thoughtfully left unlocked. Not a hair out of place in that office.'

Wide-eyed, Rose stared at me. 'Who?'

I shrugged. 'Beats me. But someone doesn't want the cops to know that anything unusual has been going on at Pallett Creek.'

'Because of the tapes,' said Rose. 'But, Jon, that's so creepy. Do you think it might be the Intelligence Agency Carl's father was connected with?'

I did not relish the thought, but conceded it might just be true. 'Have you copied the tapes?' I asked then.

'I'm almost done. I had to stop when the cops came. I've got one left.'

'Great. Then we can see about securing them. I'll go to the bank later today.'

'Okay, I'll do the last one now. Would you like some coffee and a snack while you wait?'

I flopped into one of Rose's big soft chairs. Her apartment was rather small, yet it had an air of warmth and intimate comfort I felt my larger place lacked. Indian artifacts covered the shelves and crystal and leadlight hung from the ceiling and moved soft rainbows with the breeze. The most beautiful Medicine Shield I had ever seen looked down at me from one wall.

'That would be great, thanks. I feel pretty uptight all of a sudden, I guess it's the strain. I don't know what it will be like going back to work tomorrow, after all this...thinking about Carl and wondering who...'

Rose came up behind me, leaned over and hugged my shoulders. 'You don't have to,' she said in my ear. 'I've been speaking to Curtis and he advised us officially to take a couple of weeks off, full salary.'

I sighed with gratitude. 'Really? Well, Hallelujah, praise be to Curtis. How is he taking everything?'

'Not well. I think the Pallett Creek crew are not his favorite people at the moment. At least not poor old Carl. And he sounded like he would be glad to be rid of us for a while.'

Even though I felt the injustice of such a callous attitude, I did not really care. 'That's the best news I've heard all day,' I said.

Rose gave me another hug. 'I thought you might feel that way. I've got some better news than that.' I pulled her around to face me. 'What?'

'Do you remember I told you about my aunty with the house near San Diego?' I rang her – she's not there, by the way, she's in LA at the moment. Well, she's heading off to Europe in a couple of days – she loves to travel – and she says I can have the beach-house while she's away. How would you like that?'

'I took Rose in my arms. 'I would like that a lot.'

Because of the tapes I did not stay very long with Rose. As I was leaving her apartment I saw across the street the figure of a man dressed all in black who seemed to be staring at me intently. In broad daylight, too! And at Rose's! This was too much! This was an affront! My eyes were not playing tricks on me, and I was very angry. Defiantly I stared back, then a truck drove in between us, and the figure vanished! Rose was right, this whole business was beginning to get decidedly creepy.

As quickly as I could I drove to the bank and secured the tapes in separate boxes. It gave me a good feeling to know that at least one of our problems was solved. I did not see anyone watching me and hoped that Rose was okay. I knew I would have to tell her about these phantom peeping toms, because by now I was realizing they were not illusions. The fact that they did nothing, however, was intriguing. It was as if they were trying to intimidate through fear and uncertainty. 'Okay,' I said to myself. 'I'm not as easily intimidated as that.' But I had to admit to a certain uneasiness where Rose was concerned. I did not want the creep, or creeps, hanging around under her window, scaring the daylights out of her.

Rose and I had made our plans. While I ran my errands, she was to fetch the key to the beach-house from her aunt. Then we were going to meet at Rose's apartment and drive to San Diego in her car. I would leave my car at home and take a cab to Rose's.

I arrived at her apartment, but she was not there, and I had to wait outside the building for just over an hour. All the while I kept an eye out for anything unwelcome in black, but there was no sign. Then Rose drove up at last, flushed and apologizing. Her aunt was a great talker, it seemed, and she had trouble getting away.

'I'm sorry,' she said as we went inside. 'But it's gotten so late. Should we drive tonight or wait until morning?'

'That's up to you,' I told her. 'What would you rather do?'

'I'd rather wait. It's easier to drive in the daylight, and I can make us a nice dinner this evening.' I sighed. I would have to go home again later. 'What time will you pick me up tomorrow then?' Rose's tanned face pinked. 'Oh, I thought you could stay here tonight,' she said softly.

I eyed the two-seater couch – a bit small for my long frame. 'You don't have a lot of room, and what about the neighbors?'

Rose pinked again. 'Damn the neighbors.' She gave me a secret smile. 'And you don't have to sleep on the couch or anything; I've a perfectly good bed, big enough for two.'

I did my second double-take of the day, but even while my heart was beating fast, I said the stupidest thing a man could ever utter to a woman who has just given him the invitation of his dreams, 'Rose, are you sure?'

Rose looked me straight in the eye and grinned. 'Yes, I'm sure. I wouldn't say it if I didn't mean it, now would I, Jon Whistler?'

CHAPTER 13

The Visitation

The house was old, but gracious and well preserved – a miniature hacienda of white stucco and purple flowering vines, with a wide covered patio of clay tiles that faced the ocean. I leaned out from the arched parapet and gazed down the steep slope of garden to the beach. Children ran up and down the sand; teenagers threw balls and displayed their suntans and their raw energies for one another. I suppose I had hoped for a little seclusion, but in summer, at the height of the season, that was an impossibility. San Diego is quite a popular vacation spot with many Californians. Despite being further south than LA, it has a milder climate and is a nicer city, to boot.

Rose set sandwiches and drinks on the table in the cool shade of the patio. 'What do you think of the place?'

I turned to answer, but lost her for a moment in the deep shadow; the clean bright beach had all but blinded me temporarily. Then, out of the darkness she emerged, first the lights in her superb obsidian eyes, then that Indian Madonna face I loved to look at. I was more in love with Rose now than I ever could have imagined, and it seemed that the opening of that love went hand in hand with the awakening of the capsule. I wondered if the two were inseparable movements in consciousness and had we chosen them, together, in some other dimension or time?

'Beautiful,' I said, smiling. 'Even if the beach out there is full of noisy kids.'

Rose nodded. 'It gets a bit busy sometimes, but it's a nice kind of busy, don't you think? I've had a lot of fun down there myself in the past.'

I sipped at my apple and guava juice and agreed. The colorful scene and noisy frivolity were certainly preferable to spooks in black.

'The evenings are more peaceful,' said Rose. 'I love it then...nobody much around...just the sound of the sea.'

I hope so, I thought. However I did not say it and banished the thought from my mind. I had told Rose about the unwelcome watchers, and if she was choosing to keep them out of her consciousness, then so would I.

It was not all that easy, though. At dinner our conversation managed to work its way around to who or what might be involved in trying to get hold of the tapes. Frankly, we did not have much to go on. According to Carl's story, his father had either been a Nazi or, as Razparil, something even worse. So we considered the Nazis, and Rose said she remembered reading something that alleged a Nazi infiltration at the end of the war of Western secret service organizations. Could our spooks in black be modern-day Nazis then?

After dinner we went for a walk on the beach and it was as Rose had promised, very quiet and peaceful by the lapping waters. The air was soft and mild and the smell of salt and the song of the sea stirred our senses and our blood, and it felt good to be alive. 'This is how it should be,' whispered Rose. 'When we are attuned to the Earth Mother we know Her joy in Being, and we share the joy. Then it is fit that Man and Woman should express that joy in sincere love of one another, for in the frequencies expressed and blended in the act of love, the joy is both honored and magnified and returned to its source.'

'That's beautiful,' I whispered back. 'Is that a Hopi saying?'

Rose leaned closer. 'Well, partly, but mostly Rose. Shall we go inside?' I laughed. 'Lead the way, Mostly Rose!'

Sometime in the middle of the night, around 2.00A.M., I woke up and could not go back to sleep. I had been dreaming, and in the dream had heard a call, which was, I knew without a doubt, an invitation for me to go somewhere. However, before I could discover who was calling or where I had to go, the dream faded rapidly and I jerked into wakefulness.

Rose was fast asleep and I did not want to disturb her, so very quietly I got up and headed for the coolness of the patio. I thought that if nothing else could soothe this sudden restlessness, the sea's gentle roar might just do it. Then I could go back to bed.

It was a beautiful night, very dark, and alive with those little dancing lights you often notice above a large body of water. I could barely see the slope of the garden below and the beach had all but vanished in a swathe of black velvet, so that the sea seemed quite close and almost to be singing on the doorstep. I sat out under the sky, on the patio stairs, and half shut my eyes to listen to the sound of the waves.

I must have been in a doze or nearly asleep when I became conscious of a fiery light moving from the sea towards me. My eyes flicked open, I was suddenly alert; this was no dream!

The light took form, becoming recognizable. I breathed a sigh of relief ... ZADORE. Out of the light came his familiar voice:

'Jon, I want you to pay close attention to my words. I do not wish anything I say to be forgotten; however do not fear, for before you sleep again I shall enter your consciousness in a way that will allow you to write everything down.

'I shall speak of Razparil. As you know, he was Carl's father and, after leaving San Francisco, has continued to work covertly towards the undermining of life and peace on this planet. For this purpose he formed an organization to attract the low-minded and power-seeking elements of the world, and through them he looks to dominate Mankind. This organization is dedicated to destroying the availability of greater Light and Consciousness for those who seek it. The organization calls itself 'The Order of Light and Mastery'. You may find such a title incongruous and hypocritical, and indeed it is, however it is not uncommon for beings such as Razparil and his minions to use titles like this, which will deceive Mankind and lead it astray. It is merely another form of enslavement.

'Razparil has no love for Mankind. His intentions are evil and entirely selfish. He has bartered his Light for a power that is usually reserved for the Astral Lords. Now his status is close to that of an Astral Lord and he can consciously involve the Astral powers in his work. He could have been a Fifth-dimensional Being – a Light Being – but he has chosen this current path. He could have been my Brother, but he cannot dwell in the Light unless he chooses differently. To make this other choice he must move the heavy karma, which his selfish acts continually increase.

'Once, Razparil was human, like you. And this makes him far more dangerous and effective in this world. He has stored in the Third-dimension at various locations on the Earth where he was previously incarnated, existing strands of DNA, which enable him to create a Third-dimensional body at will. Often, Astral Entities such as Razparil have maintained this dimensional contact through the process of mummification. If there are no DNA strands in a particular time or place, he then looks for any weak individual who will allow him to 'walk-in' to their body, as he did with Carl's father. In the past this phenomenon has been called possession, however possession is the wrong word because in these circumstances the host-body is always given willingly.

'Now, to Razparil's efforts to procure the transmission records, or to prevent their dissemination: 'He will use any method he can to do this. As you have realized, Carl made contact with Razparil not long after the discovery of the capsule. Razparil has agents of his organization in Los Angeles, and you became aware of them. These are your 'spooks', Jon. They refrained from approaching you because it was expected that Carl would deliver. It was they who repaired the damage to your office, since they always act covertly and are afraid to get publicly involved.

'No one can completely control another being, and this Razparil soon understood to his disadvantage. After becoming involved with the transmissions, Carl's Inner Light began to shine through the developing cracks in his darkness. So much so, that one afternoon he moved so much energy that he revealed his past connection with Razparil, thus awakening both Rose and yourself to the subterfuge. Razparil attempted to move Carl to complete his work and successfully had Carl dig up the capsule and take the tapes. However Carl's death freed him from Razparil – his death was his salvation – and now Razparil knows this.

'Razparil will attempt to gain the tapes from you in one way or another, however you need not fear.

You will exert the courage that is inherent within you, to win the battle, and you will be successful. Always remember that you are not alone – EVER!

'Razparil and his agents exert a certain power in the world and they are most powerful in the USA and in western and eastern Europe. They infiltrate all the large controlling organizations of the Earth. Governments are not free of them; their bureaucracies are riddled with them. The military, the secret services, the money controlling agencies and corporations, the media, and the so-called organizations for Peace and Health and World Unification are perverted by them. Many of the powerful and ruling dynasties of this planet have long held the DNA threads by which these manipulators of humanity can make their constant re-entry into planetary life-positions of power and privilege.

'So you see, they believe they have a lot to lose if my transmissions reach the world, and they are afraid. Beings that rule by fear are locked into their own fear patterns. They know how the message and any further transmissions will severely weaken their hold over many. It is the rebellion of individuals that they fear, as those who begin to recognize the truth of themselves will want to break free at last. The more individuals who move through the Vortex of Light and Healing, which I will send to Earth, the less power the Astrals and their minions will possess.

'If Razparil does not succeed in acquiring the tapes, he will wait until you have published and then try to discredit the message by subjecting it to ridicule through his many media lackeys. I am sure you have seen this tried before when unpopular though enlightening concepts are put forward to the public. This would be for Razparil a last-ditch attempt, as once the Word is free, It will not be constrained.

'Now, Jon, do you remember that I said I would teach you how to protect yourself from the Astral Beings when they try to force their influence upon you? I will teach you this now, and you must teach the same to Rose, as well as to all who become linked to the Vortex of Light and Healing.

'The first step is to visualize yourself as a transparent being…a transparent outline of the body. You then move this transparent form to fully encase the body of flesh. Being transparent, like a clear lens or crystal, it will allow the pure white light that you see in your mind to flow directly through, to fill the entire physical body. Watch as you create this and, as you watch, you will know that the pure white light is permeating every cell, turning each one on. You will see your whole body shimmering with this light, as it moves upwards from the base of your spine and passes out through the crown chakra of the head, to about two feet from where it cascades down, enclosing the body like an auric egg. Feel calm and safe, knowing that, while you sleep, your body will be perfectly protected from all intrusion.

'Upon awakening in the morning, before your feet touch the floor, repeat the light enclosure around your body. Then you will begin to live in your Light, with the full understanding that no unwelcome consciousness can penetrate such brightness.

'You will find that the beings of darkness will not be able to approach you to do you harm. I will be coming to you again, as well as to Rose. Remember what I have just taught, and do it every day.'

I shook myself from my concentrated state, and became aware of the coldness and hardness of the stone steps. Zadore has been here! I must tell Rose! was my first excited thought. I got up stiffly and stretched, but was galvanized into sudden action by the sound of a scream.

'ROSE!'

I dashed into the house. Rose was sitting up in bed. Her eyes were wide and her body shook. I rushed to her and took her in my arms. 'What's the matter, love?'

'OH, Jon, he was here,' she said in a trembling voice. 'Who? Who was here?'

She heaved a great shuddering sigh. 'R– Razparil. And I knew it was him, even though he didn't admit it.'

'He was here?' I repeated. I did not like the sound of that. I held Rose tighter against me, and her shudders decreased.

Then, after a moment, she said, 'He wasn't actually here. It was a kind of dream, I think. I was in another room somewhere, not here, and there were several people sitting behind a long table, as if they were judges in a courtroom. But what was strange was that they had no faces. The people were faceless! It was as if they had tight masks drawn over their faces and all that was visible were the contours. Seeing them and being near them made me shudder and I asked them what they wanted of me. They didn't reply, they just stared at me from blank eye sockets. Then a tall figure covered totally in black appeared. I couldn't see this figure's face either, because a hood covered his head entirely. I asked the same question, and this time I got an answer.

'The voice from the hood was a man's, and it sounded gentle and reassuring. It said: "We do not want anything from you, Rose. We are here to help you. We are Emissaries from the Order of Light and Mastery, and we want to protect you from the danger you are in. Your friend, Jon, is also in danger, and you must work with us so we can save you both."'

'Save us from what?' I asked. I was beginning to feel very uncomfortable in this unknown person's presence.

Rose said, 'The hooded man replied in the same soft tones. However, by now, his voice had begun to sound rather oily to me. He said: "From whom, you should ask. From the false Being, Zadore, who is an agent of darkness and would use you to promote his misdeeds here on Earth. He has charmed your senses with his magic capsule and has turned your minds away from the realities of life. His method has been to lull you into a false sense of reality in order that he can use you both like puppets on a string. Look at what he did to your friend, Carl. Carl was not taken in by this Being; he knew what he was dealing with and obtained the tapes and capsule to bring to us, so that we could stop that fiend, Zadore, from interfering with the Earth's consciousness. We would have de-activated the capsule; however, that mad daemon, Zadore, destroyed both it and Carl. I know that you saw this with your own eyes, and I also know that your friend, Jon, has a copy of the tapes. And I know that a Being of your intelligence can see through the facade of Zadore, to the evil beneath."

'I was about to say something to contradict this, but he continued, saying: "Rose, if you align yourself to this Zadore, he will destroy you, too, when he has finished with you. You must save yourself and Jon. Use your love for Jon to influence him to give you the tapes for safe-keeping and then bring them to us, and we will protect you both from that fiend. My brethren will call at your apartment to receive them. You will know them, for they will be dressed in black and will produce identification of the Order. It is essential that the future of this planet be protected, and YOU are chosen to do this. By delivering the tapes to us, you will ensure that. We will reward you both for this service. You will never more want for anything for the rest of your lives, and you will live as do the rich and famous. This, I CAN guarantee you. You will partake of all the riches this world has to offer."'

Rose continued: 'Now, listening to this, I was feeling rather ill. I thought I could smell something, too, like a stink coming from the whole lot of them in the room. I also knew that this was all upside- down somehow, and I wanted to know why, if they had no wrong reason for being in my dream, would they not show their faces? I said to them: "I don't know who you really are, or why you should have the message tapes. Zadore didn't destroy Carl; he destroyed himself. Carl told Jon and me the story of his life, and I know he did what he did because he was caught in the web of his father's evil. It is Carl's father who is evil, not Zadore. Anyway, who are you? If you are so good, why not show yourselves to me? Show me what you are. I don't believe the message of the tapes is for people who hide behind masks! What have you got to hide?"

'And that's when the man in black's tone started really to change, and he got insulting. He gave himself away then. He called you and me, Jon, "paltry humans"! He said the tapes didn't belong in the hands of such as us. He said we are all asleep to what this dimension really is, and that we really only want what They can give us! They hold our destiny in their hands and we are nothing without them!

He then said that human consciousness is nothing more than shit! Can you believe the arrogance, Jon? It made me sick to hear him go on and on. Then he started to threaten. He told me I had to get the tapes from you, or it would be the worse for me. His promises of fortune changed into threats. He said that my future would be only pain and suffering, and that I would be damned!

'That's when I called "enough"! "You can't harm us,' I said. "My ancestors will make sure of that." I hadn't thought what I wanted to say; it just came out like that. Then the man, or whatever he was, grew more angry and gave an evil laugh. "We have your ancestors trapped! Trapped in the Fourth- dimension; they cannot help you!" he shouted. I was very scared, but I shouted back: "I don't believe you! They will help. I will call on them!"

'Then the hooded man screamed at me and flung back his hood. Even in the dream I thought I would faint at the sight of him. He certainly did not live in any Light! And I knew it was Razparil – I remembered Carl's story and my intuition told me – I felt like throwing up, he was so repulsive.

'When the thing – for it was no man, that's for sure – raised its arms, I cringed. I was really frightened. I felt like a child that cries out for its mother in a nightmare from which it cannot awaken. But I wanted you, Jon. And when Razparil suddenly swooped at me like a giant bat and I felt his horrible dark and disgusting presence all around me, as if he was going to suffocate me or suck away my consciousness like a vampire, I screamed out: 'ZADORE, HELP ME!'

'Through the dark there came a brilliant Light, and Razparil let go. He screamed again, but not at me: "Begone, Daemon of Light! Do not enter MY domain!" But this only seemed to make the Light brighter, so much so that Razparil and his awful cohorts vanished. That's when I woke up and you were running in. Oh, Jon, where were you? It was all so horrible!'

Rose lay crumpled in my arms and I held her for quite a while. I told her that everything would be okay, and why. She was very much cheered by my visit from Zadore and even grew excited when I told her that she would have a visit also. When I explained the night and morning ritual to her, it was such a joy to see her relieved expression and grateful eyes.

I kissed her tenderly. 'Can you sleep now? Just do your light and know you are safe.'

Rose smiled at me. 'Are you coming to bed now, too?'

'I will, soon. As I told you, I have to write everything down and Zadore is going to help me. It won't take long.'

I left Rose and went into the dining room. With paper and pen I sat down. I began thinking I would have to try to remember Zadore's words, but almost immediately, as I put pen to paper, I started to write. The words came quickly and without pause, just as one hears of automatic writing. I knew that Zadore was writing it for me and that I was his amanuensis. As I finished, I thought to myself, Zadore has been awfully busy this night! But, Zadore, what have you gotten us into? And where is this all going to lead? What will our future be?

It was as if I heard a chuckle from somewhere in the room. 'Ask yourself, Jon Whistler, and you ask me. This is your destiny, my friend. You and Rose must remember yourselves, and carry forth the Light so greatly needed for the ascension of the planet. Remember that the Mother and her children need to escape the dark illusion which has plagued them for so long.

CHAPTER 14

The Call

As I was going to bed, the dawn of Thursday morning was beginning to touch the eastern sky with pale yellowish lights. All in all, I must have had three and a half hours rest that night and I was well and truly exhausted. Rose was sleeping heavily, too, and so we gave the whole morning a miss and woke for brunch.

Rose had a lot on her mind; I could tell by the absent way she tossed the salad, and she had spoken very little in the half hour since we had got up. I hoped she had not been too traumatized by her experience with Razparil, and said so.

'No, I'm all right, I'm over that,' she said. 'But I can't help thinking that...that thing – I can't call him a man – will stop at nothing to get what he wants, and it scares me.' Her hands were trembling, so I took the salad bowl from her and placed it on the table.

I clasped her hands in mine. 'Don't be afraid of that twisted character, Rose. He can't hurt you.

Remember how Zadore came to your rescue and how he has

taught us to use our Light for protection?'

'Yes.' She nodded, and I thought she was reassured. Then suddenly she had her arms around me, as if she was about to save me from some threat. 'It's not me I'm afraid for, Jon, it's you. I'm afraid Razparil will try to get at you too, somehow, and that he might not stop at words when you defy him.'

'You mean, attack me physically?' I asked. 'I don't think he can, my love. He and his cronies are afraid to come out into the open, to act in a way that might draw attention to themselves. And I have my Light, and there is Zadore.'

Rose sighed. 'Yes, I suppose so.'

The uncertainty in her tone puzzled me. This was not like Rose, I thought. She was usually positive and determined. So something else must have been going on inside that head of hers. 'What's really bothering you, Rose, love?' I asked her.

She went and sat down at the table, where our uneaten shrimp salad waited alluringly. I curbed my hunger pangs and sat down opposite and waited.

Rose sighed again. 'I've been having a strong feeling that I should go home to Arizona for a short while. It's like a call, you know, and it's getting stronger every day. It's happened before on occasion, when the family wants me there—'

'Then you should go,' I interrupted, although the thought of her leaving gave me pain.

'That's the trouble, don't you see?' she blurted out. 'I'm torn between yielding to the feeling and wanting to stay with you. And I don't want to leave you alone at a time like this, either.'

I did not know what to say, and the fact was that it was not my decision to make. Neither did I want to influence her, because all I really wished for was to have her by my side.

'No, no,' said Rose, as she fought the battle of conflicting feelings. 'I won't go, not yet. The family can wait. I'll give them a call, just to see if everything is okay. I don't want to leave you, Jon.'

'Okay, whatever you decide,' I said, and to my shame I must confess that I was glad.

For the next couple of days we did very little except enjoy the beach and the sea and each other.

We also used the time to discuss the future of the tapes, for getting Zadore's message to the public was our prime concern. We realized that publishing in the United States could be a problem if Razparil's influence was as wide-spread as Zadore implied, so we had to consider how easy or difficult it would be to find a willing publisher outside the country. Neither of us knew anything at all about the book industry.

To ease her mind and my conscience, Rose called her family and was puzzled to learn that there was no special crisis or other particular reason she should go home. I think that it really bothered her to believe that her feelings had failed her for once. I also felt that in her heart she truly wanted to go home, but she could not admit it to herself or to me.

To take our minds off our heavy concerns, we went to a Saturday night party a few blocks away. A woman named Joanne, who Rose knew slightly from earlier vacations, had seen us shopping in the supermarket, and invited us. Rose said Joanne was probably mostly interested in me, but we decided to go anyway.

The party was in full swing when we arrived. In fact some of the guests looked as though they had been partying for most of the day. The atmosphere was heavy with the kind of smoke that gets you into trouble with the law, but no one seemed to care. To Rose and me, though, it was not our kind of scene. 'We'll stay a while, just to be polite, then we'll leave quietly. They won't even notice we've gone,' said Rose.

Joanne latched on to me and asked a million questions until she was satisfied she knew every single thing worth knowing, then she drifted away. We did likewise, and drifted from one group to another, listening rather than conversing. Some of the conversations were weird, too. I guess it was all that smoke . 'Listen to this,' whispered Rose, when I returned with a couple of drinks. 'This guy is talking about UFOs.'

A tall thin man, with a very long nose and a huge Adam's apple and dressed like a 1960's reject, was holding court. He had a deep bass voice. 'A friend of mine photographed one, you know. And, later, he had an unannounced visit from two government guys, or that's what they said they were. They demanded he hand over the photo, but he figured they were weird and wouldn't. He asked to see some I.D. and they didn't seem to have any, so he shut the door in their faces.'

'Why were they weird?' asked a girl with curly blonde hair and startling blue eyes.

'Well, for one, they were both dressed completely in black: suits, shirts, ties, everything. Even hats! And, two, they didn't have a car, and, as he watched them from the window, they just seemed to disappear!'

This sounded familiar. Rose and I stared at one another.

The tall 60's guy continued: 'Then two days later my friend started showing signs of mind interference. Bad headaches and nausea, every time he thought about the photo. When he thought of getting rid of it, the troubles disappeared. Then he decided to get it published, and the headaches and nausea came back, worse than ever—'

The curly blonde butted in, and plainly annoying the man holding court. 'I've heard about that sort of thing. Those guys are bogus types. They aren't Earth people, they're aliens from another dimension, and they don't want us to know about UFOs, that's why they pretend to be government and take the evidence. They don't usually hurt anyone because they aren't really physical enough to do anything on the Earth, except make an occasional appearance. There's a lot of this going on at the moment.'

'Yeah,' put in someone else. 'They're called GREYS, aren't they? Aliens from another planet!'

Another girl began to speculate dreamily. 'Have you heard about the Markabians and Xenu, their leader? They've come from another galaxy to take over the Earth.'

I looked at Rose. 'Have you had enough of this?' She grinned. 'I think we need some fresh air.'

Outside, we took some time to breathe in the good salt ions and get our senses back in order. 'Let's go home,' Rose suggested. 'But what do you think about the men in black story?'

'I'm not sure, but there are similarities. It's rather disturbing,' I replied.

'Let's take a walk on the beach first,' said Rose. 'I still feel kind of stuffed-up and fuzzy from all that smoke, don't you?'

It was around midnight and I felt rather tired and drained, nevertheless a walk was a good idea. My head needed clearing and perhaps it was really the smoke and the atmosphere of the party that had drained my energies. I had watched and listened to the different people as they aired their beliefs and

I had the suspicion that their information stemmed from a sub-culture that was just a part of one more recycled illusion and was no more free of manipulation than was conventional culture.

So we walked to clear our jaded senses. It was another beautiful night. The stars glittered over the ocean and the sand was cool under our bare feet. There was no one around as we headed slowly back to the steps of the garden.

Then, just before we reached the stairs and had one last look across the water, Zadore suddenly appeared in a bright haze above the waves. It took us completely by surprise.

'Greetings,' he said. 'I see that you are amazed that I can contact you whilst you are in a physically active state. That is not so difficult; you see, the great ocean of waters has worked its magic on your consciousness and you are both now quite receptive. The manipulation of matter is quite simple, and had you, yourselves, not fallen into a sleep of consciousness long ago, you too would have been able to do more in this three dimensional world. Nevertheless, soon you will awaken to the truth of your being. I am pleased that you are now using the Light to protect yourselves from interference, but also the practice of conscious bathing in your own Light will do more than that, as you will discover.'

Rose had hold of my hand and I could feel her excitement through it. Zadore must have known it also, for his next words were for her alone.

'Rose, my special greetings and love to you. After your unpleasant experience of the other night, I am sure you have had cause to reflect on your own fears and come to some understanding of them.

They have been with you from the beginning, when you first learned of Razparil, and he used them to get at you. Had they not been there already, it would not have been possible for him to approach you as he did, for it is only the dark side of our natures that attract such as he. This dark side must be addressed. It is the garbage collected over many lives, and I do not need to explain it to you.

Everyone knows the darkness in themselves, but it is imperative that the darkness be admitted to and then actively shed. It is a task, which, if worked at with honesty and an unconditional love for self, will bring you in line with your essence self and allow the Light to shine on the Earth, through you.

'Rose, you have much strength available to you. It is in your spirit and your power of love, but it is also in your Hopi heritage. You have had thoughts of returning to your people for a time. This would serve you well now, and I urge you to consider it. I know you are torn between two attractions at the moment, but the greatest need for you personally is to choose a way that will aid in reconciling you to your higher self, and it is in the matrix of the love and wisdom of your people that you may find it. Do you understand?'

I felt Rose shiver; Zadore had touched her in the right place, I realized. Even before she answered I knew what she would say.

'Yes, I do understand, and I want to go home. But I worry about leaving Jon.'

'**A**nd in this case your worry is intuition and not the result of fear,' said Zadore. 'I want to warn you, Jon. Razparil's agents will seek you out in LA, as they are determined to have the tapes. However, if you are alert and prepared, they will not affect you.

'Now I will speak of the tapes themselves and how the publishing of them may affect your future, for I see that this has been causing you some concern. Your future is yours to decide and you have already decided some of it by choosing to honor the Message in your own hearts and by linking yourselves together in a bond of love. However, how much further you go is up to you. There is no compulsion to publish if you do not wish; you are free beings and your choices are not to be influenced by me or any other. It is now obvious that both of you are experiencing an inner awakening, and once this occurs it cannot be stopped, as your inner essence will demand that it be restored to its prime place, away from ego control.

'To publish successfully, it may be necessary to take the Message to another, safer environment, and I must warn you now that this Message is only the beginning of what is to be accomplished on Earth. If you go ahead with this initial work, I will be looking to transmit more information to follow it. The second work will be to establish the Vortex of Light and Healing, which will draw those awaiting their freedom to their own Light.

'For this extended labor you will need to live where there is less chance of constant harassment by the agents of Razparil. Jon, I want you to remember some time back when you made the acquaintance of a small publisher from Tasmania, Australia. I suggest you contact him and that he will be receptive, and I also suggest that Australia will be a safer place for you to live in during the time when Razparil's interest will be at its height. Once the work is made wholly public, Razparil will have no further interest in you both, but will only direct himself to the books.

'I must leave you now; I cannot hold the energy in this form any longer. Ponder what you have heard and decide to do what your life directs. Love to you both.'

Zadore's bright form became a general shining of starlight on the water. Lost in our own separate meditations, Rose and I watched it vanish in silence.

Australia! I liked Australia, or what I'd seen of it, but I had not believed it would come to having to leave my country for the sake of a book! But Zadore had said it, and I knew he would not say it without just cause. I looked at Rose, wondering how she might be taking the news. It was not so bad for me, I had no family to speak of, no children from my failed marriage and few relatives. However Rose had a whole network of family, and they were all close-knit too.

'Australia is a long was away,' said Rose thoughtfully.

I put my arm around her shoulders. 'I know. That was rather a shock to me, too. Let's go inside. I'm feeling beat; I need some rest after this.'

We lay in bed together, in the assurance and comfort of each other's arms. 'We'd have to give up our jobs here,' said Rose.

'True,' I said. 'But then there's the likelihood we'd be doing that anyway, soon.' Rose pulled back and stared up at me. 'What do you mean?'

'Well, a while back I read a paper from Washington that recommended closing down the Survey some time in 1996.'

'Why close it down? And why hasn't anyone told us? Why didn't you say anything?'

'I wasn't supposed to know. I saw the report by accident. I intended to try and find out if it was really going to happen, then I

140

would have told you and Carl,' I answered.

'I still don't know why they'd shut us down,' came back Rose, sitting up. 'Are you going to tell me or not?'

'Of course I am; don't get mad. The Defense Department thinks it can do our job better than we can, because it has more information on quakes than we have. They have a project they call 'SHAKE LADY', that the department reckons gives it 85% accuracy in predicting quakes and has ten times the data of the Survey. So it looks like we could be made redundant.'

'Damned military,' muttered Rose. 'But this certainly changes things. I still don't know about Australia, though.'

'Come back and cuddle me.' I pulled her down, and she yielded. 'You don't have to go if you don't want,' I said.

'Would you go?'

'Not without you.'

CHAPTER 15

Going Home

Rose was winging her way to Hopi country, and I was standing at my front door, feeling lonely and somewhat lost without her. We had decided to cut short our vacation, as Rose's need to reach her people seemed to have taken on paramount importance in both our hearts and minds, since our last contact with Zadore. It was Monday morning and Rose was already in the air by the time I had caught a cab back home from the airport.

I put the key in the front door and immediately knew before opening it that something was very wrong inside. Cautiously I let the door swing open before entering, and my heart seemed to miss a beat. The whole place had been turned upside down; it was a mess. Obviously THEY had been here, searching for the tapes.

Two waves of emotion swept over me. The first was of disgust and fear, the second was anger. 'It's going to take me days to clear up after this!' I said aloud, then that inner voice I had become so accustomed to listening to and dialoguing with of late warned me. 'Be careful of your emotions, Jon, and don't let them get the better of you. Remember to keep your cool and be prepared, because those pests are bound to turn up again.'

I made contact with Rose that night, checking to make sure she had reached her destination safely, but I did not mention the break-in. Seeing that I was okay, there did not seem any point in spoiling her visit with bad news. She was fine, and excited at the prospect of seeing her family again.

The experiences Rose would have with her Hopi brothers and sisters were to have a profound effect upon her consciousness, and since they were HER experiences, not mine, I will leave her to complete this chapter and the next.

When Jon asked me to write of my own experiences in the awakening to my higher existence, I said to him, 'I cannot leave you out of this, Jon Whistler. For fourteen chapters you have had your own way with this story of the most exciting time in OUR lives, so now it is my turn. I certainly don't intend to tell the whole story over again, but I do intend to say a few things about YOU.'

Firstly, I will say that, as an individual and a man, Jon Whistler had held a place of interest in my consciousness from quite early on in our acquaintance and long before the drama of the capsule threw us closer together. When I joined the Survey, and our boss, Alan Curtis, took me to meet my new colleagues, I felt almost instantly about Jon: 'Well, here is a genuine sort of guy who won't pull any stupid stuff with me and who I could really get to like.' And for me that was an important understanding, because as a part-Native-American woman whose looks are more Indian than White, trying to make it in a largely white, male-dominated profession had its rough spots. Aware of the troubles that were likely to come my way, I'd kept right out of the macho mining industry, and, in any case, plundering the Earth Mother for gain is not part of Hopi sensibility. However, working for the University, I was disappointed to come across a lot of male prejudice, which, although often disguised and secretive, was directed firmly at me because of my Native background. To be a woman aspiring to the worldly heights of academia was one thing, but to be an Indian woman!

And then, after half expecting another rough ride in my new job with the USGS, I met Jon and I knew right away that I'd gotten lucky. He was so kind and honest, and gentlemanly and courteous, and his respect was genuine, for me and my abilities. In our Hopi world men respect the energies and qualities of women and honor them, and women do likewise to the men. For unless we do this, how will we all survive? I felt Jon may not be Hopi, but he understood that.

So we became friends, Jon and I, and working with him was a pleasure. But I never knew he liked me enough to want to date me – the poor stupid guy. If only he had asked!

However, it has all come out right in the end – it is our destiny to be together and to share this most amazing and awesome of times.

WITH THE HOPI:

I arrived at Phoenix/Scottsdale airport and was glad to see my brother waiting for me. I had phoned ahead from LA and he had taken an hour off work to be there. Dante...that's my brother...was

working in Scottsdale for a while, and he had a place in Tempe. I would stay the night with him and his family before driving upstate to the reservation where my grandmother lives with a whole lot of my other relatives.

We had a great night at Dante's. I had not been home for four years and I had almost forgotten how wonderful it was to have the warmth of family surrounding me. Dante and his wife, Maryanne, have two little boys whom I hardly knew because they were only one and two years old when I saw them last. They were a bit shy with me at first, but they soon came round.

Then I was off to the reservation and my grandmother's village, and, very generously, Dante let me take his car because he also had a pick-up that he usually drove. As I left the built-up areas and took the highway north, I thought primarily of Jon, alone, and I wished he was with me. I also worried about him a bit, although I had talked to him on the phone the night before and he sounded okay. Yet there was something there behind my conscious reckoning that disturbed me all the same.

Arizona is very dry country. And it is quite beautiful in its own special way. I could hardly wait to see the mesas of the Hopi, and had to stop myself from pushing the foot down too hard. I really wanted to see my grandmother, too – she was the main reason for my journey, in fact. A wise old woman – a matriarch of the clan – whom I loved very much, she has been my mainstay over the years.

When I was five, my mom, who was pure blood Hopi, had come home to stay after my father died.

My father, an Easterner with a good looking white face and charm to match, had captured her heart and stolen her from her roots, but she hadn't minded then. It was not very often that a Hopi woman left the mesas of her homeland, and so, in spite of the reason, everyone was glad when she returned. I think she was glad, too, although she missed my father. However she had two young children to raise, and it was good not to be alone and unsupported.

Mom had to work, so it was my grandmother, Sage Brush, who looked after me and Dante. Well, mostly she looked after just me, because Dante, being older, was always hanging around the heels of our various uncles. At Grandmother's feet I learned what it meant to be Hopi, and everything she taught me, by example and by words, I have held in my heart and not forgotten, even when the white man's world had a way of making it take a back seat.

145

And that is why the message of Zadore moved so quickly into my consciousness, because of Grandmother and her wisdom, and the Hopi way, which is so close in understanding to the Message.

When I was sixteen, two traumatic things occurred. Mom died, and I sadly left the reservation. It had been my father's wish that Dante and I should be fully educated, and he provided us with the means in a trust. It was an opportunity that should not be lost, so I was told mainly by my white teachers. My heart did not agree then, but now I see that everything fits to a plan, and the trails we travel in our lives are not haphazard, for our higher selves have chosen them.

I reached my grandmother's place in the afternoon and my stomach was churning with excitement.

Grandmother was waiting for me and when she held me I felt like a child again, in the loving embrace of a parent. It was good to be home.

'I'm going to grind corn. Will you join me?' asked Grandmother Sage Brush.

To a Hopi woman, the labor of grinding corn is not merely an act of making flour for cooking; it can be a meditation too. I knew that Grandmother wanted to share her heart with me, and, oh, how I wanted to share mine. I had not yet told her of Jon or Zadore.

I watched her rounded body rock with the gentle rhythm of grinding – a kind of hypnotic, soothing motion, which steadied the thoughts and centered the mind. Then, as I began to mimic her, I found that the rhythm came back to me more easily than I had imagined it would.

'I have looked to your coming for many days now,' said Grandmother Sage Brush, after a while. 'Yes, I've been thinking of you. Did you dream of me?'

'I have had many dreams of you, Wild Rose.' Grandmother glanced at me sideways from the platter. 'And of another. He is older and … different…'

I felt the heat in my face as I blushed. One thing I had never been able to discount, even if I wanted to, and that was the dream-magic of Sage Brush. She was a Dreamer with no equal. 'His name is Jon,' I answered.

'He is White, and you love him?' 'Yes. For both questions.'

'It's good that you have found love, Wild Rose. But this man, what makes him so ... different? Tell me about him.'

She had called Jon different, not I, and I had thought by that she meant he was White, not Indian. But she had not meant that at all. What had she seen in her dreams?

I hesitated, not knowing what to say. Then, without my thinking about it, the words came. 'Jon is special, Grandmother. He has the heart and spirit of a Hopi, even though he doesn't realize it himself. And he has the heart of a true friend – I've never met another like him – with him I feel truly safe and totally at ease, as I am with my own self, and there are not many in the world out there you can say that about. He has a beautiful Being, though he is still unaware of it. He is handsome, too, and he is strong and kind and loving.'

Sage Brush smiled, not at me but inwardly. Then, as if she would see Jon in her mind, she raised her lined, oval face to the doorway and the blue outside. I thought how beautiful she was like that – her dark hair with its many threads of silver, her eyes so lustrous and far-seeing into spaces beyond this limited dimension. She stared into the blue and I knew she was staring into some vision of her own. She said, 'In the darkness of the Sacred Kiva, when I dreamed of you and the one called Jon, I saw the world above me open to the Sun and a golden eagle flying in its light. It is not yet the time for Kwahu to carry our prayers to the heavens, although that time is not far away. I didn't think this was

Kwahu, for the great eagle wore on its golden head a wreath of stars, and was a spirit messenger from another world. I did not speak of this to the others, for I felt that the truth of it would come from you.

What does this mean to you, and to Jon, Wild Rose?'

I ground my corn a little harder. What could it mean but Zadore? So, shyly, I began to tell my grandmother of all that had happened. I did not leave anything out, even forcing myself to describe the unspeakable dream experience of Razparil.

Grandmother Sage Brush rocked gently and ground for some minutes before she spoke again. In my flurry of excited telling I had become, on the contrary, motionless and unable to do anything but wait. Then my grandmother, too, stopped grinding.

This Zadore, he is a child of the Sun Father, Tawa, and he has chosen to speak with you and your friend, Jon? This is a very great matter to think on and I would like to Dream again. We will talk about it tomorrow; right now I ought to be thinking of our stomachs. You've come a long way to see me and I must be hospitable. I've invited Eddie and his wife, Josie, to dinner tomorrow, but tonight it's just the family.'

The 'family' meant usually seven to feed, or eight including me, and that was a big enough workload for Grandmother. The next night would mean even more. 'I'll help you,' I said. 'So let's get this show on the road.'

The next day I spent many wonderful hours in visits with friends and family. Indeed, the village was really one extended family because of the closeness of our people. The Hopi are not many, but they are strong in what makes a people survive, and that is the sense of cohesion and belonging in this often fractured world. But as for belonging and cohesion, what are they without a vision? The vision is the way of Light in accordance with the desires and motions of the Great Spirit, and was a way that could be blended sincerely with the message of Light and Healing of Zadore. This I felt as I toured my friends' homes and fields and work-places.

That evening we had a large and rowdy meal with the family and Grandmother's guests, Eddie and Josie. They were not of our particular clan and they lived in another village, but they were Grandmother's special friends from the old days, when my grandfather was alive. Eddie was an Elder of his clan and he was quite a colorful character. Josie was a small, merry-faced old lady who still giggled like a girl when she was amused. I got the feeling that they had been invited for some special purpose of my grandmother's, but I did not know what it was.

After dinner, after the children had gone to bed, we sat by the hearth and talked. Then it was clear that Grandmother Sage Brush had something particular to say. She looked at me, then at the others, then at the flames on the hearth. When she spoke it was with authority, with the power of direct understanding.

'The Hopi, like other Indian Nations of North America, still await the coming of Pahana, he who we call the Lost White Brother. We know he is not the same as the white people who came and, through their greed, took from the Indian a land that was not theirs to take. No, Pahana is not of their whiteness. Pahana is white, like light. It has been written that he will bring with him symbols, as well as the missing piece of the sacred tablet, which is in the safe-keeping of our Elders. This piece was given to him when he left, and the return will make the tablet whole again. This will create a healing of all the Nations, and this we pray for.'

Grandmother paused to draw breath, and the others nodded and murmured amongst themselves. All this was well known to us, however everyone liked to hear it again.

Grandmother continued. 'Now, yesterday brought my granddaughter, Wild Rose, back amongst us, and glad we are that she is here. She has brought with her a message of hope, as she told me of a Being of Light who has come to her through a mysterious capsule, and in the waking state and not through dreams. I have thought about this deeply and last night entered the Dreaming to discover more. In my dream I journeyed to the Sun and there met this Spirit Being of Light, who appeared to me as an eagle crowned with stars. I have previously seen this Being in a vision in the Kiva and believe that this is the messenger of Taiowa who will bring us the joy of a new world. Our clan has been blessed, for it has been chosen to carry the message of the Fifth World to the Nations of all colors and races.

Tomorrow I intend to take Rose to a meeting of the Elders, so that they can be witness to the coming of Pahana.'

Eddie and Josie and the others had listened intently while Sage Brush spoke her understanding.

There was much nodding again and some comment, then Eddie began to question me at length about the capsule and the Being of Light. I did as I had done for Grandmother, only leaving out the more personal references to Jon, and when I was finished he patted my hand in a fatherly way and chuckled, saying, 'I knew Sage Brush was up to something tonight! But this does your clan and all the Hopi great honor. We shall celebrate your message – all the clans shall celebrate the joy you bring us this day.'

I hardly knew what to say. I felt shy and pleased all at once. I gazed through the open window at the sky. All the stars were alight and blazing like diamonds, and they seemed to be focusing their brilliant eyes on this one place on Earth tonight.

CHAPTER 16

Zarine

The evening of the following day, when I would go with Sage Brush to the meeting of the Clan Elders, seemed a long time in coming, as everything does when you wait for it with nervousness. I wiled away the hours helping my grandmother with her chores and watched as she worked at some of the Hopi crafts that bring needed dollars into the reservation. I could not help with those because my craft skills had gotten rusty over the years and my fingers were now too inept and clumsy to produce first class, saleable work. But I enjoyed the quiet peace of her company and we gossiped of trivialities and laughed a lot and, of course, we talked about Jon. Grandmother Sage Brush wanted to know all about him: how old he was, what he looked like exactly, his history. She was keen on meeting him. 'Just to check him out,' she said, and hoped he would want to come to Arizona soon. I hoped so too, for that would properly round out my life, I thought – Jon here, with Grandmother and the family.

I did not say to Sage Brush that the next visit might be the last one for a while. Even knowing this was a possibility, I did not want to discuss that then, not even with myself.

After dinner with the family, my grandmother dressed herself in her best clothes, and I dressed in mine and, carrying a few small gifts for the Elders and their wives, we made the short walk to the house of one of the Elders. The main living area of the house had been swept bare of everything and the four Elders sat cross-legged on a beautiful woven rug on the floor in the center of the room, while their wives were sat together on another at the side. When we entered, (I trailed my grandmother inside) they all nodded and smiled and gave greetings, and immediately I felt less nervous, for these people were all our friends.

'Nice to see you, Sage Brush. You have something important to tell us?' said one of the Elders. 'I have brought my granddaughter here. You know Wild Rose, she is the one with the important news,' said Sage Brush. 'She has returned to the clans with a Great Vision, and to seek guidance and await your response to what she has to tell you.'

The Elders nodded to me to speak and nervously I told my story for the third time. They sat and listened intently, and never once interrupted. They waited to hear all of what I had to say without putting their own opinions or interpretations forward. It is very common in western society for people to only half listen to what you are saying before they jump in with their own ideas. And they are often more interested in downgrading what you say, since they feel their own opinions are more important.

I said my piece, and there was absolute silence. The Elders made no attempt to discuss what they had heard but seemed to be in meditation, as they allowed the meaning of the message to sink into their consciousness. Hopis do not think initially from the head, or intellect, as most Europeans do. Reason and logic are subservient to intuition for the Hopi and therefore they are able to grasp the core, inner meaning of an issue much more quickly and, to use a fashionable term, holistically. I knew I would have to be patient and sit the meditation out, so I closed my eyes and relaxed.

As I waited I thought primarily of Jon and, for the hundredth time that day, I wished he was by my side, with his hand in mine.

'Wild Rose.'

My eyes flew open. The oldest Elder was addressing me. He was a withered, once-strong-looking man of about seventy-five. His 'white' name was Vernon.

'You have been given a great Vision, one that will complete the Prophecy, which has been kept sacred by our people and is carved on Prophecy Rock. The Day of Purification is at hand, when it will become necessary for all the people of this Earth to choose which way they will travel – the true, straight path of our creator, Taiowa, or the zigzag path, which leads to destruction.

'It is clear to us that you have been chosen to help fulfill the destiny of our Nation, and that in sharing this honor with a man of the white race, you do the will of Taiowa, which is that there be peace and harmony and understanding between all the Nations of the Earth.'

The Elder gazed at me from steady, kindly eyes. A slight smile creased his sun-browned face and his eyes twinkled as he acknowledged me and my Vision.

Then the second Elder spoke in a strong, deep, very solemn baritone voice. He was called Robert, but was known generally and familiarly to the children of the village as Unka Bob. I remembered that he was not usually so serious and that he had a reputation for humorous pranks. He said: 'The Fourth World shall soon end and the Fifth World will begin. Pahana will come again – the Man of Light – and he will restore the missing part of the Sacred Tablet. We will hear of a dwelling place in the heavens above the Earth that shall fall with a great crash, and is the abode of evil spirits who wish to join the battle of the Earth Mother. There will be confusion across the Nations, but Pahana will prevail.'

The third Elder followed on Unka Bob's heels, saying: 'There will be a great turmoil, as the men of many nations fight amongst each other, for they need the power to try and conquer the Earth Mother.

They shall explode their great bombs and smoke shall rise into the sky, and its message will be easily read. The rocking to and fro of the land will produce great changes to the Earth Mother herself, but as Pahana unites the Nations, he will save those who follow the straight way of Taiowa.'

This Elder's 'white' name was Jethro, and he was the serious one amongst us. He was a big man who did not smile much, and I had always been in awe of him.

Then, finally, the fourth Elder spoke. I knew him well, as he was a cousin of my mother on her father's side. He was the youngest of the Elders, and I realized with a shock that he was only about five or six years older than Jon. A handsome, virile looking man, who wore his hair in the old braided way, he went by the name of Kai. He smiled at me gently when he spoke to me.

'Wild Rose, your Vision has been confirmed and your Destiny seen and acknowledged. You will go with our blessing as you carry the dream of our Nation into the Fifth World. Perhaps your journey will take you to far places, to other Nations, but eventually you will return and sit with Us, as one of Us. Elders will no longer need age to gather wisdom, it will be born into those of the Fifth World.'

Now, Elder Vernon took over again. He nodded to my grandmother and me and said, matter-of- factly, 'Tomorrow evening we make a special ceremony, so that all may share this great Vision.' Then he winked at me. 'Then we have a big dance and we all have a great time. Wild Rose, you get all dressed up, not in those white woman's clothes though. Then you make all the young men wish you weren't already spoken for.' He laughed good naturedly and the other Elders and their wives and Grandmother joined in. I blushed and laughed with them.

The next evening, in the Sacred Kiva and before many representatives of the clans, the Elders conducted the promised ceremony. It was not like any of the usual ceremonies, but contained some of the elements of them. It seemed to me that Vernon and Unka Bob, Jethro and Kai had chosen not to plan the ceremony out but depended rather on following the guidance of the Great Spirit, which was their Higher Self speaking to them. Except for giving me the special gift of a power bundle, they moved the ceremony on with a kind of hesitant but graceful spontaneity, and everyone was allowed their chance to speak if they wished. I knew the facts of my Vision had already been circulated around the reservation, so everyone was clued in on what this ceremony was about. Many men and women rose and spoke the joy of their hearts to me and to the others and then a meditation followed. I sat there, overwhelmed and nearly in tears, because of the wonderful spirit which pervaded the hearts and minds of these, my good gentle people.

When we rose from the meditation, I was presented with my bundle. It was a piece of soft rabbit skin and it held four special objects. There was a small pouch, which I knew contained the sacred corn meal of the ceremonies. This was never to be eaten, but was used ritualistically for spiritual cleansing and blessing, as holy water is used in the Christian churches, perhaps. The first Elder opened the pouch and, with three fingers, sprinkled some of the white meal on the floor in front of me and around me. Then carefully he marked my forehead, cheeks and chin with it.

The next object was a paho, a thread of cotton from which hung the golden down feather of an eagle. This the second Elder handed me.

The third object, given to me by the third Elder, was a tiny kachina doll with the mask of a Soyal Kachina. I understood that it represented new life, and guessed that its symbol of the rising sun had been chosen for the apt purpose of representing the new world to come.

Then Kai presented me with a small weathered shell. A spiral seashell, which had been worn around the neck of an ancestor from the mysterious South, when the world was different from today. Holding it reverently in my hand, I could see in front of me the endless tides of Humanity in the long journey from the Source. I knew that this little shell represented the history of the migrations of our people, but it also seemed to me to symbolize a vortex in its spiraling design.

Then the ceremony was over and we all went outside into the still, bright evening. A huge fire had been lit in the square, and its vermilion flames leaped into the magenta sky, casting warm orange lights on the excited faces of everyone. There was feasting on trestle tables in the square and, when that was done, a dance. It was not a dance like the European Americans have, of course, and it was not a dance of a particular ritual or ceremony either. But it was very special, because it moved with the rhythms of ceremony and it drew those who danced into the sacred movement and meaning of the spirit.

Two circles of dancers wove around the fire, one circle clockwise, the other in the opposite direction. I danced in the inner circle, my hand on the shoulder of the dancer in front and the hand of the dancer behind on my shoulder, so that we were all connected. The dance was hypnotic and the rhythm of the drums, bells and rattles moved one outside the world of everyday.

Like the other dancers, I danced with my eyes closed and unconsciously and in attunement with the rhythms, as I moved into a resonance with the inner spirit. As I danced, my legs were tingling, as if a thousand ants were running up and down them. This sensation surged upwards into the rest of my body, then I felt that those who were holding my shoulders had thrown me into the air!

I opened my eyes and saw that I was flying head first into the sky. It was like being catapulted off a cliff, but I knew I would not fall. In front of me flew a magnificent pure white eagle, and I followed it, soaring.

I gazed down upon the Earth. It looked dark, with many villages appearing burnt-out and destroyed. The people looked sick and hungry. Some glanced up and, seeing me, reached up their arms for me to lift them up. But I could not.

On we flew, my white eagle and I, and again I looked back to the Earth. It was now covered with water and all the land masses protruding above the water were massive volcanoes shooting molten lava and ash into the atmosphere. The surrounding water bubbled and steamed from the intense heat.

We flew further. Onwards through a rainbow, and suddenly the land below changed. There were many villages and no sandy wastes. The Earth was green, all covered with fresh sweet grasses, and there were animals grazing. Everyone seemed content, concentrating on their tasks, and they did not look up.

I glanced from the Earth back to my white eagle, but it was no longer there. It was then that I became caught in a spiraling vortex and, in this vortex, the dancers were rotating in opposite directions, creating a movement of tremendous energy. The dancers had become the vortex.

At the center of the vortex was no fire, but a woman of great beauty with the definite features of an Indian. She had two white feathers in her hand and these she gave to me. As soon as I took them, the form of the Indian woman began to change, as it emitted brilliant colors, until it was as bright as the Sun.

Then I realized that my form was glowing until it mirrored the other. From within this atmosphere of intense Light a voice spoke to me:

'You are Zarine, mother of the Earth energies, and I am your Light in the Fifth-dimension. You followed your Light and Fourth-dimensional consciousness here as you witnessed the misery and destruction and, finally, the rebirth of the Living Earth. You, Zarine, through the union of your inner dimensional beings, shall work to lead others through the Vortex of Light and Healing, and, in so doing, shall lift the Earth energies. The time draws near for the Earth to ascend in consciousness.'

Suspended inter-dimensionally, I felt the union of my consciousness blend through all three dimensions, and my being was filled with peace and light. Time did not exist any longer, everything just WAS, as it WAS and IS.

I awoke on the Third-dimension and found myself lying on the ground with the other exhausted dancers. The dance was over and now each dancer lay at peace, experiencing the frequencies that the dance had created in them.

For the rest of the evening until quite late, there were other dances and still more feasts. But no other dance gave me the thrill of the first and, besides, I was too overwhelmed by the experience of my integrated selves to want much more activity. I found I was content to watch more often than dance, and to listen with closed eyes to the changing rhythms of the music. And my mind was in other realms, with my white eagle self and with Zarine, who was also me.

On the following day I told my grandmother of my experience at the dance.

Sage Brush nodded and took my hands in hers. Her eyes were full of love and joy, and she said, 'Wild Rose, you have a great destiny, and I see it taking you far from this village. But know that my heart will always be with you. I am an old lady now, so I don't know if I will be able to see you in the Fifth World here. But I certainly will from above. The evil spirits do not control our destiny as they think they do, for there are many people who try to live the truth. Know that when you leave here, it will be with my blessing, and I trust that you will have great happiness in your life with Jon. I hope that I will meet him before you travel afar.'

Tears started in my eyes. I knew that in a couple more days it would be time for us to part. Parting with loved ones is always difficult, and especially with those who we may not meet again in the physical body. However, if we only miss the body contact, then that is not so important, as the Light Body is eternal and links us all together for eternity.

'We still have a little while together, and I do promise to bring Jon here to see you,' I replied, giving Sage Brush a great big hug.

On Monday morning I said my farewells to the whole village and drove mournfully back to Tempe. And as I got closer to Phoenix I started to cheer up again. After all, I was going to spend a few more pleasant days at my brother's house, getting to know my nephews better, and then it was back to Jon!

Jon! I could hardly wait to see him. I wanted to tell him of my experiences, but chiefly I wanted to tell him how much I loved him. The time away had strengthened my feelings for him enormously, because being apart from him made me realize how much I wanted him in my life. Even my old home, as much as I loved it, did not seem to complete me or wholly satisfy me, whereas Jon's presence did.

I had been phoning Jon regularly from the village store – Grandmother did not have a phone – but they had been quick little calls to see if everything was okay. I had not phoned since Sunday morning and I wanted to tell him what my plans were, so at Tempe on Monday night I gave him a call. But I could not get an answer. I tried several times before it got too late, but had no luck. I was disappointed, but there was no choice but to wait until Tuesday morning. I knew he had gone back to work from Monday on, so I decided to ring early, before breakfast.

However, still no luck. No answer at the apartment and none at the site office either. I reasoned that somehow I was managing to miss him every time; nevertheless, I was beginning to feel uneasy. When the phone just rang and rang on Tuesday evening, I felt my heart leaping in my breast with fear.

Something was wrong, I was sure. But what?

CHAPTER 17

One Light

While Rose was away from me I seemed to exist in a kind of Limbo land between my thoughts of the amazing past weeks and my ever present considerations of the future. In my heart I knew that the future would take care of itself, and my heart told me not to worry, but I was still having considerable trouble with my head, which continued to dream up endless scenarios of possibilities. 'Old habits die hard,' as the saying goes, even when we are able to recognize them for what they are – that is: patterns of behavior, which have been ingrained in our consciousness over aeons of time.

Once I knew Rose was with her Hopi clan, I ceased to worry about her safety. And, besides, she called me every day, so the contact was comforting, even if rather brief because she could not talk openly or intimately in front of the people in the village store.

It took me two and a half days to clean up the mess in my

apartment. However, that was not the fault of my unwelcome intruders but rather because it stimulated me into making a complete overhaul of all my stuff. It was a kind of cleansing process, I guess. I threw out a lot of useless, old items, things I had been clinging to needlessly over the years and were associations with a past I did not want to bother with any more. I felt in myself that it was a freeing of the new Jon Whistler from the old and, as I did this, it seemed that a lot of emotional baggage got tossed out with the junk as well. I did not go out much during that week and every night I kept a watch at the window for any sign of Razparil's agents. They did not have me scared as such, but the knowledge that they were not likely to give up on me was disconcerting. It surprised me that there was no contact attempted and no sighting at all. Maybe they're playing a game with me, I thought. They hope that by keeping out of my way they will make me nervous enough to crack.

Tactics like this were a distinct possibility, I decided. Nevertheless, damn it all, I was not going to cooperate with that! It was time to get on with life and ignore these guys, at least until they made their move. So on Friday I climbed out of my shell and called Head Office to see about getting temporary replacement staff to help me at the Site. 'Sorry, no can do,' said Alan Curtis. 'The budget has been cut and we're not replacing staff.'

Feeling I already knew the reason for this, I waited to see if he would make any attempt at explanation. But he did not. When I asked a probing question he fobbed me off with evasive excuses and hung up. 'So that's how they're playing it,' I said to myself. 'It's pretty clear then that I'm going to have to make some decision about the future soon.'

Monday arrived and I left early for the Site. It was strange to be going there knowing that neither Rose or Carl would be around. Still, the loneliness gave me time to think, and I must admit that I had little enthusiasm for the work and spent a lot of the hours going over my finances in my head and thinking what it would be like to leave this country for another. I was not terribly anxious to go to Australia, although when I had been there before I had quite liked what I had seen of it. I wondered how Rose would feel about going, especially after having been home for a while. I would understand if she did not want to leave and I certainly would not try to make her. Neither would I leave her behind; I would just have to stick it out here, no matter what.

Financially speaking, I was not too concerned. I had never lived high and had saved quite a bit in the ten years I'd been on my own. I had a few investments, too, and I owned my less-than-new car, and I knew that the pay out from the Survey, based on my entitlements for long service, would be a good one. They would not balk at paying it either, I guessed, because it would save them in the future, when redundancy time came around.

It was hot slow work that day, and the day seemed longer than usual with no one to talk to. By 4.00P.M. I'd had enough of the dust and sweat, so I trekked back to the site office. I felt weary as I made myself a cup of coffee, and decided to go home as soon as I had tidied up my desk and logged in the day's work on the computer. I was thinking of Rose and hoping she would be back soon, when I heard a car pull up outside.

'That's strange. Who could this be?' I asked myself. Perhaps it was the cops with all the stuff from Carl's desk. I glanced through the dusty window, to see a black Taurus parked nearby. The thought crossed my mind that you don't see all that many black cars these days, then it hit me. 'It's THEM!' I said. And then brave, unflappable Jon Whistler panicked.

There was a knock on the door. I cursed myself for not being prepared, especially after the last week at home. I went to the door and opened it. To my surprise there was only one person standing there – a small, thin, weedy man who looked as though a puff of wind might easily blow him over. But who, or what, was he?

'Mr. Whistler?' the man asked.

'Yes,' I replied. 'What do you want?'

He was dressed from head to toe in black. His suit was

immaculately pressed and clean and his shoes gleamed like two black mirrors. He stared at me from eyes that were very narrow slits and were protected by thick goggle-like glasses. He smiled in an insipid manner.

'I am from the United States Investigations For Alien Contact. The late Mr. Carl Reisenger contacted our office some time ago, reporting the discovery of an object that may have some scientific significance. May I come in?'

I did not see that letting this joker in the door would make any difference to the situation, so I said okay. But I left the door open wide just in case there was a problem. He was such a scrawny little weed though, who did not seem capable of giving me much trouble, and his skin was so deathly pale that I thought he must live under a rock. Even with the door wide open the office was very warm with the late afternoon sun beating down on it, however the strange little man showed no sign of heat or perspiration, in spite of his hot, black attire.

'You have some identification?' I asked.

He whipped out a badge of some sort with a photo attached, flashed it in front of my face and put it away quickly, before I could tell what it said or whether the photo was of him or not. 'So this is the game, and there ain't no rules,' I said silently to myself.

'Well, to be quite honest with you, Mr...?' I said.

I waited.

'Plant,' he replied.

'Mr. Plant. I haven't a clue what you're talking about. I know nothing of any...object, did you say? You know that Carl Reisenger blew himself up and that he was probably mentally disturbed, so I don't think it is wise to believe anything he may have told you. He obviously had problems of some kind and may have been trying to draw some attention to himself.'

If it was at all possible, the man's eyes thinned even more as he seemed to look right through me. He said, 'I have not come all this way for nothing, Mr. Whistler. Our organization knows all about you, Mr. Whistler. And it knows that certain audio tapes are involved with this event and we believe you have them. It would be best for you if you handed them over to me, in order to save any further investigation into your affairs. It is not wise for you to become involved in something about which you have no knowledge. You are skating on thin ice, Mr. Whistler.'

Do these guys ever give up? I thought. I said to him with as much force as I could, 'Look here, I've told you I don't know anything. You are wasting your time coming here. Maybe, if you're serious about this, you had better take your enquiries to the Survey Office and talk to the powers that be about Carl and whatever else.'

It was obvious that I had pushed the right button, for the little black weed glared at me and replied, 'We do not want to involve too many others in this, as this is a matter of government security. Now, Mr. Whistler—'

By now I felt that I had the upper hand, so I jumped in on him. 'LOOK PAL, I've already told you once, and you're wasting my time as well as yours. I have to shut up shop now, so I think you had better leave.' I pointed to the door.

The pale little man did not budge, and he stared at me through the slits of his eyes. When he spoke his voice had an edge of ice to it.

'This is not the end of it, Mr. Whistler. We will talk with Ms. Medlin, and I feel sure she will be more cooperative. You had better watch out, for you may have a very serious accident in the future.'

I felt the anger rising. Damn these creeps! 'Get out or I'll throw you out!' I almost shouted, and I moved towards him.

Without a flicker of fear or any emotion whatsoever on his face, the cold blooded little creep merely turned and walked out the door. 'You leave Ms. Medlin alone!' I shouted after him. I found I was sweating and shaking with emotion myself, whether of anger or because of the fear that THEY might try something nasty with Rose. Perhaps it was an arrogant male assumption, but I did not consider THEIR trying something with ME. All I could think of was to protect Rose from the evil, and since I had her brother's phone number in Tempe, I decided then and there that I would try and contact her as soon as I got home.(9) I did not want to frighten her, but it was preferable to her being unprepared.

Wiping the sweat from my face, I collected my things and left the office. As I drove the rough road to the highway, I worked out the best way of warning Rose.

At the last turn of the track before the highway, I rounded the bend and almost ran smack into a black car that straddled the track. I swerved and hit the brakes, but my car tires failed to grip on the loose gravel and I went into a slide. I left the road and catapulted into a deep ditch, then WHAM!

No air bag in my old car. My ribs hit the steering wheel and my head whacked the front window with such force that it was little wonder that I did not smash through the glass. Then darkness took me.

I woke up and saw that my car had ended up tipped forward and sideways into a ditch, with one back wheel spinning. The black car had vanished and there seemed to be no signs that it had ever existed. I wondered how I had gotten myself out of the ditch, and then I looked closer at the wreck. A body was slumped across the steering wheel, and it was mine. OH JESUS, I thought, I'M DEAD!

As this thought flashed through my mind, a dark swirling mass descended on me. I felt imprisoned, trapped. Then I heard a sinister, evil laugh echoing in the darkness, and I knew whose laugh it was.

RAZPARIL!

'Foolish little being, you can never escape now!

'Look at you, dead to the world! And once you leave the Third-dimension, your ego and your consciousness as Jon Whistler will cease to be! Your Fourth-dimensional consciousness is fast asleep to all that is you, Jon Whistler, and it is useless for you to continue in the attempt to liaise with Zadore, for he too cannot help you any more. FOOL, what was the use of your hiding the tapes? They will never see the light of day now.'

I was lost; I did not understand. It seemed that I had a body exactly the same as the one crumpled in the car. I could still feel the same body sensations, I did not feel any different from before. So what did Razparil mean that my ego would cease to be? And what was my Fourth-dimensional consciousness? And how was it asleep? Was it beyond the radiation belts?

I could not see Razparil. 'Where are you? Show yourself!' I called. Then I wished I had not asked, for from the darkness his monstrous apparition appeared. Carl's' story of his experience flashed in my mind and I winced, remembering the evil that this being had done to the child, Carl.

'Petty being,' snarled Razparil. 'You have now entered my domain, and it is your dark side that holds you as a prisoner here. However, if you would leave this level of your own darkness, if that is what you desire, then only I can help you leave it.'

Just looking at Razparil made me feel ill. 'What can you do?' I asked, although I could see nothing good or helpful coming from this direction.

'First you must tell me where you have hidden the tapes, and then, and only then, will I free you from this eternity of darkness. That is all you need to do.'

I was so caught up in misery and panic that it did not occur to me that Razparil's words were now a contradiction of his earlier speech. After my experiences with Zadore I felt I had made a contact with my Light that could not be sundered, yet here I was, sunken in a revolting darkness and the only apparent way out of it was to do a deal with a demon from Hell!

It was then that I thought of Rose. My God, if Razparil found out that she knew where the tapes were…! Or did he know that already, and would he attack her too, if I did not cooperate?

'Oh, Rose, Rose. Is our love and happiness to be so cut short?' I said to myself miserably. The thoughts and sorrow enclosed my consciousness and temporarily blanked out Razparil, for I was now in a dimension where when I thought of some emotion I experienced it in all its intensity. I could see Rose vividly. She looked radiant and happy, talking and laughing with an old Indian lady whom I felt was her grandmother. Rose! I tried to touch her with my mind and tell her what had happened. I needed Rose

166

now. I felt sudden despair and this jolted me back into the macabre realization of the moment.

'Where are the tapes?'

'No…no!' I fought the unclean intrusion of the demon into my consciousness. Then a voice within me spoke, and I knew that my familiar inner voice had not left me. The voice reassured. 'This is only a trap; you are not really in darkness, it is only the illusion of the Dark One. Negate the darkness and send it back to its own dimension!'

Bravely I faced the evil countenance of Razparil. 'I will call on the Beings of Light to cast you aside. I am not of your making, and you will never have the information, because it is the Message of Light, and I call on my Light to expel your evil illusion!'

But Razparil did not vanish. Instead he threw back his monstrous head and laughed and laughed, so horribly that I was truly afraid.

'Ha, ha, ha! YOUR LIGHT! YOUR LIGHT! Your Light, as you call it, is asleep! Asleep on the Fourth-dimension, where IT has been trapped by our power for a very long time. Once your Ego turned away from It, It became captivated by a web of dreaming and fell asleep. Puny, petty Ego that you are, you have NO power over ME! You crippled weakling, you know nothing and you are now a part of MY darkness!'

I did not want to believe this, but I could find no answer but a dumb, wordless shaking of my head.

Razparil seemed to delight in my agony, for he laughed again, even louder.

'HA, HA! Fool! What you little realize is that I AM YOUR SHADOW! What you think about me that so disgusts you – that is not separate from you. YOU ARE A PART OF ME! You think you have Light with Zadore, but I am HIS alter ego. I AM YOUR DARK SIDE— now you are MINE!'

'No!' I screamed. 'It is not true!'

I was desperate. I thought I would blubber like a child. Instead I called out to Zadore, 'Bring your Light to this darkness, please!'

'Paltry words!' shouted Razparil triumphantly. 'Nothing can

save you now. You are MINE— FOREVER!'

I watched helplessly as Razparil raised his arms, and I knew he was about to engulf and suffocate my consciousness in his infernal darkness. He oozed a foul aroma, like something rotting, and surrounded the whole Ether with great darkness. I felt that his triumph would be to possess my Ego and, with it, the DNA of the Third-dimensional body lying in the wrecked car. As a form of self defense I directed my consciousness inwardly to what I knew was still my higher being. I felt the spiraling chakras moving in unison and a surge of energy moving through my etheric body, which, at the moment, was only me.

A strong dark energy battled me, pulling against my attempted ascension. Then, through the crown chakra of my head, a brilliant light burst out and upwards.

Razparil screamed then. He screeched, not at me, but at the Light: 'How did you escape? How did you awaken?'

The Light, which even now was taking on the form of a man-like being, proclaimed: 'This prisoner of your dark side awakened me, and now you lose. You cannot hold any of us prisoner again. My Light will clear all darkness from this etheric plane. Depart, Demon, forever into your dark abode— I, SIZZOND, command you, for this is not the realm of darkness; it is only your illusion.'

The Light of the Being, Sizzond, expanded and grew so much brighter. I heard a horrible scream. Razparil's red eyes glared at me from what was left of his hideous form, as it evaporated like mist in the sunlight. Then they too disappeared.

I looked at the one, SIZZOND. It was so beautiful a being, and was neither female or male in particular, but combined the expression of both frequencies in one form. Grace and strength, tenderness and power, a form of supple lightness and harmony. Who was it?

A smile beamed from the beautiful face. 'Do you not realize who I am? I am Sizzond – your Fourth- dimensional consciousness.' Before I could reply, something began tugging at my shoulders. I heard voices.

'He's alive, he's breathing. Let's get him out of this.'

CHAPTER 18

Into The Vortex

Shadows danced across the screen of my closed eyelids, then one descended upon me. I felt the pressure of something that covered my nose and mouth and I received a fresh rush of oxygen into my lungs. Then there was pain as I was dragged clear of the car, and I was gently laid on somewhere soft and carried. Doors slammed, an engine started up, a siren screamed. I knew I was in an ambulance, on the way to LA and hospital.

My consciousness wavered between numbness and pain. My chest hurt, my head spun. Then a brief sharp spasm of agony shot its electricity through my body and was swiftly followed by a strange dullness of all sensation. I was spiraling outward from my body again, out of the ambulance, out of the Third-dimension, and I was not sure of where I was going or to what.

'What are you searching for?' asked a pleasant voice.

I looked directionally around me, except that there were no directions in this place. No left or right, up or down, but only

169

pulsating frequencies of light. It was then I saw Sizzond.

'How did I get back here?'

'You never left,' was the answer. 'You only returned temporarily to your physical body, which still acts as a vehicle for your Third-dimensional consciousness. Whether it will remain so depends upon what you must decide now. Your body is having difficulty in maintaining its attachment to you, and if you sever the connection of your Light, it will cease to be.'

'What!' I exclaimed. 'I don't think I can get used to being dead!'

'Well, Jon,' replied Sizzond. 'You are still connected to that body by a golden thread of consciousness and your Life Vortex is still in place. If you leave the Third-dimension, then that etheric mass of frequencies, which you currently consider to be you, will eventually disintegrate, and the morphogenetic patterns of your memory fields will flow through me.'

I was not sure I liked the sound of that. 'If that happens, what will become of ME?'

Love and compassion filled the glorious face of Sizzond. 'That, which you call 'me', is only a lens – an ego frequency, which allows the flow of the REAL YOU to manifest on the Third-dimension, in a body. It is a temporal thing. Once it disintegrates, your consciousness will become a part of me, for I AM YOU on the Fourth-dimension, just as YOU ARE MY CONSCIOUSNESS on the Third- dimension.'

I could not cope with all of this. 'How can I be what I am talking with? I don't understand,' I said to Sizzond.

Sizzond smiled. 'Jon, all consciousness moves through the dimensions of creation, and everything is and is of Light. Consciousness adapts to the altered frequencies of the dimensions by using the energy packets, or bodies, to experience and express the dimensions back to Light. Just as you are my frequency on the Third-dimension, so I am the frequency of Zadore on the Fourth-dimension. As we move back to Light, our consciousness moves through(11) our consciousness entities on the higher levels of Being.'

I was still somewhat confused. 'Am I going back to the Earth dimension or returning to your frequency?'

170

'We can decide that quite easily, Jon,' said Sizzond, 'for, as you know, both you and Rose must move through the Vortex of Light and Healing of Zadore.'

Rose, I thought, as the light of love flowed through my etheric frequencies. Oh, Rose, I can't leave Rose, not now.

Sizzond interrupted my reverie. 'You must return, Jon. However do not forget this experience, for it was you who awakened my frequency on the Fourth-dimension, after it had been lulled into a sleep- like state by Razparil, so that he could dominate the lower levels of our being. He had caused me to move into a frequency of bliss and ignorance, such as you had experienced on the Third-dimension. Zadore found that he could not move his consciousness to the Third-dimension through me, so he had you find the capsule. As such, he has been able to communicate with you directly from the Fifth- dimension. And now we are one beam of Light, and we are moving the Light of the higher dimensions to the Third. THE VORTEX HAS BEGUN.'

There was something else I wanted to understand, so I asked Sizzond, 'How was it that Razparil moved your consciousness into the sleep-like state?'

Sizzond nodded. 'There is much that the Third-dimensional consciousness is unable to comprehend. Zadore is a Fifth-dimensional Light Being and, as such, can in no way be affected by the consciousness of the Astral Fourth-dimensional entities. Zadore's consciousness has been manifesting on the Earth dimension for many thousands of years. During the early times, before the Astral entities interfered with the Earthly realm, I have focused Zadore's Light through the many different Earth bodies, and I had retained the same continuing ego consciousness. Jon Whistler has assumed other names throughout the centuries, but always while responding to the same higher frequencies.

'Well, that is not quite accurate, since for many, many aeons until now, you, Jon, have tended to turn your back on your higher energies, and this turning away of your Ego from your Light to the Astrally- created Illusion is what lulled my consciousness into sleep.

'Until these recent times, Razparil has held a dominating influence over your Ego, although you were ever unaware of it. Through you and many others in the Third-dimension, he has used and still uses his power of control to achieve the ambitions of the Astral Lords.

'With the Vortex of Light and Healing, others like you will move their Egos toward the higher consciousness that is within each and every being on the Third-dimension. This is the true purpose of the Vortex, for it will quickly lessen the power and illusion of the Astrals.

'Razparil has no Third-dimensional body at this time – the old German, Carl's father, died some years ago(10). So Razparil is concurrently working through the many thousands of egos, which he controls. His karma is so great, especially in regard to what he did to Carl Reisenger and his father in his quest for power and domination.

'Razparil's current effort in regard to you was to try to move HIS consciousness into YOUR EGO, and back into Jon Whistler's body. Then, had he accomplished this, he would have destroyed the tapes and would have worked to lead Rose's consciousness into his own evil pattern. However, because Zadore has been focusing his Light directly through (11) you, he has been moving your Ego self to directionally reflect Light, and this is what defeated Razparil. For Razparil underestimated the strength of the Fifth-dimensional Light that Zadore had blended into your frequencies, and your remembrance of me.

'Razparil is basically an Alter Ego of what was once all of us at one time. As Zadore told you, Razparil could have been his brother on the Fifth-dimension, only he chose otherwise. He has no more power over you or me now, as we are one with Zadore. He will continue to vampire other

bodies until he becomes weakened in his energies, and the Astral Lords will cast him aside. This will take many thousands of years, and his evil presence will haunt the Earth for a long time yet.'

I began now to worry that if I did not get back to my Earthly body, then this etheric body would disintegrate. So I asked Sizzond how long it would take.

'About seventy-two hours of Earth time. However your attachment is still quite strong, Jon, not only for the Vortex of Light and Healing but also for Rose. Nevertheless, it is essential that you return soon, before your body develops any brain damage, which would lessen the effectiveness of your contact with the higher energies. There was some damage – some concussion to your head – but it will not present a problem and will heal completely. It is time to go, Jon. Go in my peace and love.'

Once more I began to rotate and spiral through the darkness. I was aware this time of passing back through the Life Vortex, and gradually became conscious of Earthly surroundings and Earthly light. I peered downward into a dazzling set of walls, a polished floor, and a hospital bed surrounded by a gleaming mass of complicated technology that seemed to be chattering away contentedly to itself. In the bed, and wired up like one of the glittering machines, was a pale, corpse-like figure with a bandaged head. Someone was sitting by the bed and holding the left hand of the unconscious figure.

I gazed on the scene below me. I could see that the two people were very connected with one another because the auric fields that surrounded them were blended almost into one flow. One aura was substantially more vigorous in expression than the other and seemed to be flowing its energy into the other, which was gradually gathering strength. This flow was, I knew, the devotion of my beautiful Rose, as she poured all of her love and healing into me.

More than anything I wanted to be with Rose. So, THUD, I landed. I felt my body jerk, and pain began to radiate from centers in my head and chest.

For a while after I lay in a darkness of pain and emptiness. I tried to open my eyes, but the light in the room seemed blinding. Then, gradually, I eased them open. My vision blurred, adjusted to the light and focused, and I looked up into the wonderful obsidian eyes of my love.

With all my strength I squeezed Rose's hand. I managed to whisper, 'Hi.'

Rose jumped. Her face cleared to a glorious smile, although her eyes instantly filled with tears. 'Oh, Jon, you've come back!'

'Couldn't keep away from you,' I would have liked to have said, but nothing more seemed to come out. For maybe half a minute I gazed at Rose and smiled, and then, very gently, I simply drifted away. Not into unconsciousness, though, but into a sleep that was free of pain. I did not know then, of course, that this all too brief contact was to throw Rose into a state of panic, because she thought the worst was happening. It was only after the doctors checked me out and were able to reassure her that I was on the road to recovery that she calmed down and, finally, after hours of waiting stoically by my side, went home to get some sleep of her own.

I don't know how long I was asleep, but during that time I experienced a beautiful contact with my higher Light energies. Both Zadore and Sizzond came, and they were not as separate entities, but were blended into each other somehow, into one magnificent Being. And Zadore spoke to me:

'We are all ONE now, Jon. The Vortex is complete. You have become the Vortex, as all Light flows through us through all dimensions. Rose, also, is now blended as one consciousness, and you are joined in the Vortex. It will now begin. What you will understand and experience is that your Third-dimensional body will heal very quickly, as all energies flowing through the Vortex will align all the disturbed frequencies within you. This is the way of the Vortex, and the way of the future. You will feel no more those negative insecurities, and will move the energy of the Vortex across the planet, both Rose and yourself!'

When I awoke in my hospital bed, Rose was not there. 'Gone to have a well-earned rest, but she'll be back soon,' the nurses told me.

I did not mind waiting. My pain had lessened enormously and I was feeling hungry. When I asked the nurse if I could have something to eat, she stared at me, astonished, but shrugged and ran off to see if it would be okay. My quick recovery astonished them all in fact, and I only wished then that I could have told them plainly why. But telling would have to wait until I could get the Message out to the world, and now I was so eager to accomplish this that I was impatient to be up and about. It took me a week to get better, and that was long enough.

And all the while, Rose was my constant and loving visitor. We used the time to tell each other of our special adventures and visions, and we discussed our future options regarding the publishing of the transmissions.

One subject I did not broach was the one of leaving the country; I decided to save that up until I was back at my apartment. When Rose came to pick me up from hospital, I found that I had to squeeze into her car in between a whole lot of her personal bits and pieces.

'Well, after what's happened to you, you don't think I'm letting you stay alone in that big old place by yourself, do you?' she said, when I asked about her stuff. 'Someone's got to look after you; so I'm moving in. I hope you don't mind.'

With a determined, don't-argue-with-me expression on her face, she started the ignition. 'Of course I don't mind!' I exclaimed. 'Rose, you can look after me forever, if you want!'

Rose let the engine die. She turned to me and smiled quizzically. 'Jon, is this some kind of proposal?'

My heart did a leap. 'Yup. The best kind,' I said sincerely. 'Rose, I love you – I will forever. And I want to spend my life with you. I don't want to live without you, Rose. Will you—?'

Her arms flew round my neck and she cut off the rest of my words with the hottest kisses I have ever received. I kissed her too, then she murmured in my ear, 'Forever, Jon, forever.'

EPILOGUE

When I was properly strong again I went back to work. I had to; there was no other way of paying the medical bills, which, in spite of my having insurance, were still horrendous. Rose returned to work on the same day and because of the USGS cutbacks we became a team of two, and I must say that we rather enjoyed ourselves during that time before we eventually quit the Survey.

Life was not without its tensions, though, for my 'accident' had made us wary and kept us continually on the alert for any further attempts to prevent the eventual publication of the transmissions. It was this that decided us finally to go with the suggestion of Zadore and seek a publisher and a temporary home outside the USA. Since Rose and I had joined our hearts and minds and selves together, and after all the amazing things we had experienced, choosing to leave the familiar for the unknown did not seem like such a big step after all. For, did we not have each other and the Light of our own true natures and a message which would change the world?

So, in the months that followed, we set ourselves to work towards bringing the Message of Zadore into a form that everyone could share. It took me a while to figure out the way of presenting the transmissions that would attract readers and keep them reading and, afterward, thinking. I could merely have printed them as they were and presented them on their own, but somehow a story was needed to put them into an understandable and human context. 'Why not just write about everything as it happened?' was Rose's suggestion, and this seemed the best idea.

Therefore, all I had to accomplish then was the overcoming of my own inhibitions regarding myself as a potential author. But the egotism of authorship and literary accolades are not what this book is about. It is the Message that matters, and only that, for the Message itself, if felt and understood with heart and mind and applied to every moment of our existence, will take us beyond the Ego and the limited view it represents, and we will find that we do not need the praises or approval of a world that is asleep to the true wonders of Being in Light.

Following completion of the book's manuscript(12), Rose and I made a wonderful journey to Arizona and Rose's family. Meeting the venerable grandmother was my greatest expectation and concern and I was somewhat nervous about the event. I wondered what she would think of me, whether I was suitable for her granddaughter, that I was too old and too foreign maybe, that I was stealing Rose away from her people. I felt that going to see Grandmother Sage Brush was like going on a pilgrimage to a holy shrine. I expected great ceremony and formalism and perhaps a naturally understandable distance between us because of our conflicting cultures. I must admit that all I truly knew of the Indian was through Rose and of Rose, and the rest of my understanding was stereotyped in that regard.

So what a wonderful enlightening surprise when we finally met! Rose and I arrived at Grandmother's front door in the late afternoon, with the immense reds and golds and blues of the dwindling desert day as our backdrop. On me, the views of the desert and the little villages set within it had a sobering effect. I thought of universal vastness and how small and insignificant seemed the outcrops of humanity, yet how harmoniously and how triumphantly they could live within the vastness, if they tried. I guess that made me feel a certain awe for this separate world, and I was prepared, like Rose, to venerate it too and, along with it, the most respected grandmother.

Sage Brush was a small, round-looking woman with bright black eyes and silver threads in her long black hair. I had expected someone older in appearance and, in particular, I had not reckoned on the wicked merriment of that venerable face. I say this last on purpose, because she reminded me very much of Rose in that way. After brief introductions, Sage Brush ushered us inside out of the heat, hugged Rose for a second time and then offered us cool drinks. Then she proceeded to inspect me.

She asked me a number of questions about myself and nodded as if she was fairly satisfied with the answers. She asked me if I had fully recovered from the accident and I said yes, I was fine. That seemed to please her greatly for some reason. Then, saying something in Hopi to Rose, she walked over to me and whacked me very firmly in the stomach, said something more I did not understand and sauntered off into another room!

Stunned, I stared at Rose. 'What was that for' Have I done something wrong?'

But Rose was laughing from behind her hands. 'No,' she said. 'Grandmother really likes you, a lot.' 'Then why did she hit me? And what did she say?' I asked, bewildered.

Rose laughed some more. 'Are you sure you want to know?' 'Yes.'

'Well, to paraphrase, she said that you look like a real sexy guy and that you are in a fairly good condition for a man of your age, but that you had better stay that way, if you're going to be a good husband for me!'

So once I had the approval of the grandmother, I then had to meet the clans and the Elders. This occurred at a formal, though friendly kind of gathering in which practically every Hopi from miles around seemed to be there. Apparently, Rose and I were big news, or rather it was the Vision that the Hopi Nation looked to that attracted them, and we were but the esteemed harbingers.

A few days later the four Elders: Vernon, Robert, Jethro and Kai, took me on a trip to Prophecy Rock. Rose and Sage Brush did not come, for the reason that Rose told me was that the Elders had effectively adopted me into all the Clans, and it was an honor that I should go alone with them to this special place.

And I was honored too, as I stood in silence in front of the monolith of stone while Vernon explained the meanings of the symbols carved upon it. When he was done, there was another general silence, then it became clear to me that the four of them were waiting to hear what I would say. I had no trouble expressing my feelings for the prophecy, for I immediately saw the similarities to the Message of Zadore, and felt a recognition in my own heart.

'Mankind has two futures that may be chosen – a light-filled, healthy one, if the truth of Being is adhered to and honored – but if the other, selfish way is chosen, then only destruction will ensue.'

They were satisfied with that and were pleased, they said, that I had come with Rose to see them. Then Vernon took from his own neck a chain of golden, sun-like stones and gave it to me. The stones were uncut topaz and by their polished beauty and the well-worn chain, I knew that this gift was very old and cherished. I accepted the gift for what it meant, to me and to them.

In conclusion, Rose and I present one more transmission. This was received by us in 1995 and is directed to you, the reader. I will say no more, and will allow Zadore to speak the final word:

'GREETINGS.

After having read this book, you will realize that it encompasses the need for personal remembrance of your true state, not for any selfish reason, but for the future of the living planet, Earth. Once you move your consciousness away from the Illusion that has wielded control of the Egos of self for many thousands of years, you will, in a natural manner, beam the Light of the higher frequencies back to your physical Third-dimensional body. That is all that is required of you, for, in so doing, you are giving the Earth the Light for its movement into the Fourth-dimension.

That is what the message is about. You must re-read the transmissions several times and take the message into your consciousness, whereby you will then personally be able to move into the Vortex of Light and Healing.

Reflect on the experiences of both Rose and Jon, for they, too, represent the road that your Ego must follow also. Their experiences will not be your experiences. But you must discard all the negative luggage of those past lives your Ego has lived in the Illusion, negating your Higher Selves on the Fourth and Fifth-dimensions.

Some of you will find the transmissions a purifying experience, which will catapult you into the Vortex that I have prepared for you. For others of you it will mean a need to desire the Light above all and throw off the past karma that holds you back. The Vortex is a growing dimension of Light, and as you purify and enter the Vortex, you will add to the power of it.

I will be sending more information to both Jon and Rose in the future, that will form a basis of a working manual for you to move your consciousness into the Vortex. The Earth will not be hindered by the Astral Lords again, for we will, in mass, move the Light of Light into the consciousness of the Earth, and we will destroy the Illusion of Darkness forever.

Love and Light of Light be with you forever!

Sizzond Zadore in Light.'

ENDNOTES:

Chapter Two:

(1) When the Earth moves from being a Third-dimensional consciousness to that of the Fourth- dimension, those human beings who are still locked into the Third-dimensional Illusion of the Astrals and who are unable to make the shift in consciousness that the time demands, will move to another planet of Third-dimensional density. At the same time, the Astral Lords, who currently habitate in a small part of the Astral-dimension, will be exposed to the higher consciousness of the Earth and its inhabitants. As such, their Illusion will be rejected and they, too, will be unable to continue to function in their negative state. They, too, will be moved into the realm of the Third-dimension with those humans who still cling to the Illusion and its time-loop. Those who make the shift in consciousness will be beings dwelling in the realms of Light and Love, assisting the birth of the Earth's new bodies.

Chapter Three:

(2) It must be seen that the Earth Children will be the consciousness produced in the formative elements of the Earth matter, that are currently being seeded by beings such as yourself. By raising your consciousness and moving to the greater Light of your being, you are seeding the DNA of the Earth. This will eventually produce Egos that will link them to the higher frequencies of the Galaxy. You are not of this planet, but are Light Essence from many Star Systems throughout the Galaxy. The Earth beings will grow in consciousness on the Fourth-dimensional Earth.

(3) Here the Earth transmission once more relates to the manner by which the Astral Lords attempted to store higher frequency energies in order to break free from their prison. Stone structures were built over many thousands of years to store

energies from the Sun and other Stars in the Galaxy. These were stone circles and pyramids, such as those now found in Great Britain, Egypt, China and the Americas. Natural rock formations on the Earth constantly store energies from the Galaxy and radiate altered frequencies to all plant and animal life around them. The Earth is both a receiver and transmitter of energy. Fortunately, the Astrals were unable to accumulate sufficient energies from these formations to move them out from the Astral belts around the Earth. Later, though, they were able to use these structures as ritual sites, to draw on human energy.

Chapter Four:

(4)   In this transmission, the Sun continues to elaborate on the relationship developed between the Astrals and Humans. The Soul of Man is the Ego. This concept has been expressed in many writings. It was the Ego that turned its back on its Inner Light and, in an unwritten agreement with the Astral Lords based on the promise of greater power, used the Illusion as a means to control matter. It no
longer wanted to listen to the voice of Light, but only the voice of Reason. That, which is looked on as being the Soul – the Feeling nature of the Ego – exists in a limbo state, or sleep state, abandoning its Light Body on the Fifth-dimension. You regain your consciousness of your Soul and Light Body when you become, once more, One Light!

(5)   Here the Illusion is well described and also your involvement within it. It is seen as Life exposed to all uncertainties, and such uncertainties are considered as being the real you. The greatest part of the Illusion is that you consider that the body you inhabit is really you! From this stems the fear that, should something occur to the body, such as sickness, pain or death, this will be the end of your consciousness and all that you are! The Illusion is seen as presenting you with things that are considered as being real, such as power over others, creating illusory entities such as: Governments to rule and provide for us; Churches to provide our spiritual needs and salvation; Science to develop super-drugs to keep our bodies alive, and other gadgets

to make life more livable; and your own deception, where you deny that your Inner Essence is as real as your body pretends to be.

Chapter Five:

(6)   Upon later advice, the initials used previously to indicate certain names have now been removed. J.W. 2004

Chapter Six:

(7)   Here the Earth concludes its dissertation, and states that it is only through 'ME' (the Earth) that you will once more find again your Soul and Light Bodies. By moving away from the Illusion and desiring to give your Light to the Earth, as you initially decided, you will once more develop contact with your Soul Essence on the Fourth-dimension and your Light Body on the Fifth-dimension.

Chapter Ten:

(8)   The Vortex of Zadore was created to provide the means by which you can now move your Ego into direct contact with your Essence on the Fourth-dimension. As you move into the Vortex, the energies within it will begin to burn off the karma that has been accumulated over many lives on the Earth, and free you of the Astral control.

Chapter Seventeen:

(9)I now have some memory of being enough worried about Rose that I tried to contact her from the site office but could not get an answer at the number she gave me. So I decided to wait until I got home. Rose has since informed me that she and her nephews and sister-in-law had gone out for ice- cream and didn't get home until 5.30P.M. J.W. 2004

Chapter Eighteen:

(10)I have since discovered this to be incorrect. Razparil had not left the Third-dimension at that time, although the body he inhabited was very, very old and near to its termination. My only excuse for such a mistake is to say that this contact with Sizzond was experienced whilst I was in a situation of extremity. Everything that happened on that Monday was temporarily confused by the car crash and had to be wrenched from memory later on. The experience between the moment of the crash and the time of my regaining full consciousness had to be recalled and reported also at a later date, as it was not given to me in the way that the transmissions were. If the error was mine or Sizzond's, I cannot truthfully tell, but am inclined to attribute any incorrectness to my own failure of understanding under the circumstances. With this in mind, I have scanned all of this chapter and all of the previous one, searching for any additional failures of memory or inaccuracies of expression or understanding, but have found only two...as follows:

Refer Chapter 17. Endnote (9) and
Chapter Eighteen (11): This should be 'to' not 'through'.
J.W. 2004

Epilogue:
(12)The main bulk of the manuscript up to this point.

GLOSSARY OF TERMS:

Ascension:

Ascension is the transformation and movement of a conscious entity to higher frequencies of Light. Currently the Earth is in the process of its ascension from the frequency of the Third-dimension to that of the Fourth-dimension. Such a frequency shift will create different life expression on its surface, which will be born out of all that currently exists in this Third-dimensional environment. This includes all plant and animal organisms.

Astral:

The Astral is another term for the Fourth-dimension. It consists of a range of frequencies that commences after the higher Third-dimensional frequencies – the Etheric – cease, and moves to the point where the Fifth-dimensional frequencies commence. The Astral frequency of the Earth is contained between the radiation belts and the surface of the Earth. All Third-dimensional planets in the Universe have Astral frequencies surrounding them. The Stars like the Sun, Sirius, Pleiades, etc., are not surrounded by Astral frequencies, as they are Star Gates to the Fifth-dimension. However, all the planets in their solar systems have Astral frequencies.

Astral Lords:

These are being who once dwelt on the Fifth-dimension and who were imprisoned in the Astral field of the Earth by the Galactic Lords. They were imprisoned there for their transgressions in the Galaxy subsequent to their war-like tendencies, which they have continued to impress through illusion on the Human Ego. In old literature they were called 'Fallen Angels'.

Astral Entities:

These are those Human Egos who have turned completely from

their Inner Light and have taken on many of the negative frequencies of the Astral Lords. They continually disrupt human society on Earth by occupying areas of power and control.

Ego:

The human Ego is a permanent frequency of the One Light. It exists on the Fourth-dimension and moves all consciousness through the Third-dimensional Earth Body. It is a dual Essence that is controlled by an Intellectual Polarity that dominates and suppresses its Feeling Polarity, or Soul. As such, it directs all of its energy outward through the five senses of the body.

Illusion:

The Illusion is all that is felt to be real in the Third-dimension. Such realities rely on sensual experience as providing the ultimate in happiness and power, and are seen as being the highest point of creation in the Universe. The Illusion is a creation of the Astral Lords, which dominates the mind of Mankind. The Illusion is the reality of man's existence, whereas the Earth and its elements are the actuality of existence.

Light Body:

The Light Body is the 'Higher dimensional self', which is currently fragmented throughout several dimensions, due to the Ego focusing its frequencies mainly on the Illusion. Once you turn your back on that Illusion, you will link all those frequencies that are uniquely you.

Radiation Belts:

The Radiation Belts are energies that are of a similar frequency to those of the Sun. They enclose the Earth and contain all the Morphogenetic patterns that the Earth requires to develop frequencies that provide vehicles to express higher consciousness. The inner belt contains all the information or history of the Earth itself. It will reveal all information to those who seek to understand the Earth Consciousness.

Gain greater understanding and light by reading these other titles available from Light Pulsations

ENTER THE VORTEX AS ONE LIGHT
ORACLE TO FREEDOM
THE THREAD OF INFINITY
FIRE ON THE SEA

THE VORTEX PAINTING

This painting was created especially at the behest of Jon Whistler as an expression of the Vortex of Light and Healing and as a focus for medication. It is offered as a high quality full colour print 40 cm x 40 cm in size.

For further information email us at
lightpulsations@gmail.com

http://www.lightpulsations.com

Made in the USA
Las Vegas, NV
24 October 2024

10410077R10108